# THE FOUR LEVERS OF CORPORATE CHANGE

# THE
# FOUR LEVERS
# OF CORPORATE
# CHANGE

## PETER L. BRILL
## AND RICHARD WORTH

## amacom
### American Management Association

New York · Atlanta · Boston · Chicago · Kansas City · San Francisco · Washington, D.C.
Brussels · Mexico City · Tokyo · Toronto

Library of Congress Cataloging-in-Publication Data

Brill, Peter L.
      The four levers of corporate change / Peter L. Brill and Richard
   Worth.
         p.      cm.
      Includes index.
      ISBN 0-8144-0339-5
      1. Organizational change.    I. Worth, Richard.    II. Title.
   HD58.8.B753    1997
   658.4'06—dc20                                              97-9320
                                                                 CIP

Printing number

10 9 8 7 6 5 4 3 2 1

# Contents

# Foreword

In 1492, when Columbus set out across the Atlantic Ocean and landed in a new world, his voyage changed the perspective and literally broadened the horizon of every European. Almost overnight, trade routes had to be redrawn, power began shifting from the Mediterranean to the countries on the Atlantic seaboard closest to the Americas, and great riches began flowing onto the continent from places with unusual sounding names like Pitosi and Tenochtitlán.

In many ways, the corporate leader with a new vision is like Columbus and the other explorers who came after him—people who change perceptions. But it isn't easy. For years, no one was willing to finance Columbus's voyages; and it was only his sheer persistence that finally enabled him to transform his vision into reality.

Today's corporate leaders face similar problems when they try to implement their vision of change. Change forces employees to shift paradigms because it upsets the tried and true ways of doing things; it produces anxiety and stress by requiring employees to learn new skills and deal with unfamiliar situations; it also threatens many employees by upsetting traditional power relationships and lines of authority. Is it any wonder, then, that as a leader announces a new change initiative, managers smile and nod their heads approvingly, only to return to their offices and sit on their hands? Is it also any wonder that so many change efforts fail?

Suppose you run a large manufacturing firm. Business has been declining recently because competitors have been introducing new products into the marketplace much faster than your company and luring away customers. You have some specific ideas for reversing this trend, so you call together your management team to discuss them. During the meeting, several of your department heads express strong support for your proposals, but there are two key players who seem less than enthusiastic. The Vice President for Operations sits silent and stone-faced throughout the entire discussion. And the head of MIS, while agreeing that a change of direction might be necessary, sadly explains that his staff is already overworked and "cannot possibly take on any additional responsibilities." You desperately need the cooperation of these two highly talented department heads to make the change effort succeed. What's more, they must work together. Unfortunately, they are intensely competitive and they have instilled this same attitude in their subordinates. Over the years, both leaders have built up their own fiefdoms in the organization, and the last thing they intend to do is give up any power. How do you handle this situation and initiate the change effort?

*The Four Levers of Corporate Change* provides a framework and guidelines for solving this type of problem and many similar ones that regularly confront anyone who leads an organization. The book explains how to deal with those aspects of *human nature* that motivate employees to resist change; it provides fresh insight into the uses of *power* to initiate the change effort and keep it moving forward; it offers a new, more realistic definition of corporate *leadership;* and it explores the dynamics of *social processes*—the engine that provides momentum for change. Thus, the authors give us many practical and insightful answers to the question: How can we make change succeed?

Today, given the increased complexity and uncertainty of operating in the global information age, all of us in the field of management are looking for principles that can guide organizations and enable them to be successful in the future. This insightful and innovative book, based on years of practical experience, incorporates some of the unchanging laws of human nature, power, and social dynamics; and applies them in the arena of corporate change. I am convinced that the book will give you a new perspective on your role as corporate leader and a set of principles that if employed will increase your ability to cope and navigate your way through the turbulent business environment and create the needed organizational changes.

The book—and its focus on effective change—is a natural addition to the research stream of the SEI Center for Advanced Studies in Management—the "think tank" of The Wharton School at the University of Pennsylvania—on the question of: "What are the critical characteristics that organizations should adopt if they want to flourish in the 21st century?" As such, the book is a must-have guide for any leader who faces the inevitable need to change and create value through change.

Jerry Wind, The Lauder Professor and Director
of the SEI Center for Advanced Studies in Management
The Wharton School, University of Pennsylvania

# Preface

Today's leaders face incredible problems. Staying abreast of the accelerating rate of change, motivating employees, obtaining reliable information, competing internationally—these are only a few of the balls that managers must keep in the air as they try to run organizations. The rate of technological change alone exceeds anything that seemed possible only a few years ago. Employees are more highly educated than ever before and demand greater empowerment from their bosses. Time is a far more valuable commodity—time to market and just-in-time inventory. The global economy affects major business decisions, from cutting health care costs to opening new factories. Finally, customers have much higher expectations from the products and services they purchase; thus, no company can afford to overlook quality. Faced with such a variety of complex issues, organizations often look for one-dimensional solutions. Everything from TQM to reengineering becomes "the answer."

## *The Four Levers of Corporate Change*

In this book we take a more realistic look at the complexity of organizational management and work toward real-life solutions. The book describes the major areas where organizations most often need to change and why a single one-dimensional answer usually fails. But knowing *what* needs to be done is not sufficient without knowing *how* to make it happen. Therefore, we examine in considerable depth the four key factors that enable the change process to be successful.

First, we examine *human nature* and how to persuade employees to work for, not against, change. Second, we discuss *power,* a subject that most executives are even more reluctant to talk about than their sex lives. Properly used, power can make change succeed; misapplied, it can destroy a company's entire effort. Third, we explain how to use *social processes* to initiate change and give it momentum down the road, overcoming pockets of resistance. And fourth, we describe the *role of the leader* in evaluating human needs and motivations, developing a social process based on them, utilizing power to make that process work, and creating employee identification with the change initiative to keep it running in the future.

Based on extensive interviews with more than 1,000 senior executives conducted by Dr. Peter Brill's colleagues at the Wharton School, our book begins by describing twelve essential characteristics for pace-setting organizations in the twenty-first century. We then explain how to use the four levers of change to help organizations acquire these characteristics: for example, how to become more cross-functional, flatter and empowered, networked, stakeholder-focused, customer-driven, and innovative. We would like to acknowledge our debt to Dr. Jerry Wind of Wharton for developing the twelve hallmarks of outstanding organizations.

Finally, we conducted interviews with CEOs at leading organizations to determine where their change efforts were succeeding and failing. This information, combined with our own extensive consulting work with corporations, enabled us to design a book that is reality-based and geared to the needs of today's business leaders.

Because we believe that the problems besetting modern organizations are timeless, we begin each chapter with an appropriate historical anecdote. Then we use examples from our own consulting practices and interviews to demonstrate how to use the four levers of change most effectively. Finally, we apply these levers to help organizations acquire the hallmarks of success.

Chapter 1 introduces the complex issues that are not susceptible to quick fixes or silver bullets. Anyone who works inside an organization or runs it knows that there are problems that must be grappled with if the change process is to work.

Change often begins with a crisis. And Chapter 2 discusses the role of crises. A crisis in an organization often acts as a catalyst for large-scale change. Alternatives that may have seemed unthinkable only a short time earlier suddenly appear eminently practical. The book illustrates this point through a case study involving a health maintenance organization. We also explain that if a crisis doesn't exist, sometimes a leader must create one in order to galvanize the change process. The best example is Jack Welch's actions at General Electric.

Chapter 3 points out that many change initiatives begin with an idealistic vision. However, many vision statements also contain principles that are too idealistic and too specific, and when some of them later prove to be unrealizable, employees grow skeptical and disillusioned with the change process. It is better to begin with only one or two basic principles and add others later.

Chapters 4 through 7 form the heart of the book: Each of these chapters discusses one of the four levers of corporate change:

1. Understanding of human nature
2. Skillful use of power
3. Well-designed social process
4. Persuasive leadership

A lever is a very powerful tool, despite its simplicity, and the four levers we describe can initiate positive change in almost any organization if used correctly.

Human beings lie at the center of every change effort, and throughout history many have put up strong resistance to it. During the nineteenth century, for instance, the English Luddites saw their livelihoods jeopardized by industrialization and tried to stop it. There are Luddites inside every organization, and they will derail the change effort if you let them. Leaders must learn to mitigate the impact of natural human traits—suspicion, stubbornness, and anxiety—that undermine change, while capitalizing on those positive human qualities—trust, idealism, and dedication—that make change work. Chapter 4 discusses some principles of human nature and how change leaders can apply them.

Another key attribute of any successful leader is knowing how to use power effectively. However, power can be misapplied, producing gridlock and failure. By contrast, Chapter 5 presents several critical elements that characterize the skillful use of power, applying them in a case study involving a financial services firm.

Chapter 6 examines the importance of a social process in initiating change efforts. The chapter defines social process as "a series of events or experiences that utilize our knowledge of individual and group behavior to facilitate change." Effective social processes are aimed at transforming employees' belief systems; therefore, they must win over not only the mind but also the heart of each individual. Properly designed social processes can take full advantage of elements such as cognitive dissonance and the power of consensus. Case studies illustrate how a social process can produce change.

No change effort will succeed, of course, without skillful leadership. But leadership involves more than a list of traits and attributes. As described in Chapter 7, leadership of the change effort is a clearly defined process that includes information gathering, self-knowledge, identifying the informal leaders inside an organization, developing a realistic set of ideals, finding the leverage points to induce change, understanding human nature, using power effectively, designing a successful social process, and creating identification with the change effort among rank-and-file employees.

Chapter 8 focuses on the importance of alignment and identification to keep the change process on course. Although Mikhail Gorbachev knew how to initiate change, he was unable to persuade Soviet citizens to identify with his new programs. As a result, chaos and fragmentation ensued. This chapter identifies several elements that lie at the foundation of the identification process that can prevent the fragmentation and failure of a change initiative.

The last chapter explains how to use the four levers to introduce the hallmarks of leading twenty-first-century organizations. It explains how to determine which hallmarks may be most important in your organization, how to work on several of them simultaneously, and, once you have successfully used the levers to introduce change, how to keep the process running properly.

For many years we have worked with these issues. Peter Brill has dealt with them as a psychiatrist who proceeded to attend business school, management consultant to many *Fortune* 500 companies, fellow at The Wharton School, and CEO of his own business, all of which have enabled him to develop a variety of successful techniques for managing organizational change. Richard Worth is the author of ten books, as well as a communications consultant for major organizations. Together we have written a book for CEOs, managers, and consultants based on practical experience, a book that we hope will guide you in successfully changing your organization.

# Part One

# A Framework for Change

# 1

# There's No Silver Bullet

On a steamy July day, the leaders of a major American organization assembled at a stately old colonial building to discuss the serious problems currently confronting them. They were operating in an environment that was daily growing more turbulent, with increasing economic pressures from abroad and dissatisfaction among their domestic customers, and the organization itself was rapidly being torn apart by fierce internal struggles between its various units. Indeed, disaster seemed in the offing unless the organization could somehow change.

Not all the men assembled that day would be considered charismatic leaders, or perhaps even great speakers. Nevertheless, they represented some of the best minds any organization could bring together. The chairman was a retired general, a man who had the universal respect of everyone in the room, but who was often austere and, some said, even icily cold in his dealings with subordinates. Nearby slouched a rotund figure whom everyone simply referred to as the Old Man; well past retirement age, he had stayed on because he had a profound knowledge of the domestic and international landscape, as well as the uncanny ability to tell a story that could instantly bring laughter to his colleagues and defuse the tension that often developed when they met. Other executives in the room that day included a ramrod-straight New Englander, known for his incisive analytical skills, a handsome *Wunderkind* from New York, considered a genius in finance, a courtly Pennsylvanian who had lost a leg in a riding accident, and a tall, handsome Virginian who would dominate the early part of the proceedings.

As the meeting progressed, it soon became clear that there was a profound disagreement over what types of changes needed to be made in the organization. Some of the men in the room favored nothing more than a little tinkering with the current systems, but others were just as

3

adamant in their belief that the entire structure needed to be overhauled. One of the first to propose a comprehensive plan for restructuring was the Virginian; he outlined a new power-sharing arrangement between the central administration and the individual operating units. Since these were of different sizes, this plan would inevitably favor the larger ones—a fact that was immediately pointed out by someone from one of the smaller units. "I do not, gentlemen, trust you," he told the representatives of the larger units, daring to say openly what was on the mind of many of his colleagues. And it wasn't long before they came up with a counterproposal that called for more balance between the units, which would be competing for power and scarce resources within the new organization.

Meanwhile, reports of the meeting had already begun appearing in the press. So far reporters knew little more than that an event of profound significance was under way, but it wouldn't be long before they would try to dig out more. If reports of dissension leaked out, it might undermine the public's confidence in the organization. Let the outside world believe that great progress was being made in the deliberations and that everyone assembled was unanimous in the new course the organization should follow. Of course, nothing could have been further from the truth. Already there were two plans on the table, and a third was currently being proposed by the young financial genius from New York.

The wrangling over competing blueprints continued for some time. And it was only because of a compromise offered by the New Englander that an opportunity to break the deadlock finally presented itself. Still there were numerous other issues to debate: the degree of empowerment for each member in the organization, for example, and the amount of authority that should be placed in the hands of a central planning body. But most of those attending the meeting were united in recognizing that their organization faced a profound crisis, and that unless they could agree on a plan to deal with it, the future for all of them and for everything they had worked so hard to build was extremely uncertain. It was this spirit of compromise, as well as the influence of the Old Man and the chairman, that eventually forged a framework that would prove successful.

While this could be a description of a meeting occurring today at a major corporation, of course, it isn't. Instead, it is a description of a gathering that took place during the hot summer months of 1787 in Philadelphia: a convention of leaders who created the United States Constitution. The Constitution has been called by some "the great experiment" and by others, including a few of the Founding Fathers themselves, the "miracle at Philadelphia." This great democratic document emerged because the men who gathered during those stifling summer days refused to become "prisoners of their context," slaves to the rules and regulations of society as they found it. Instead, they mastered the context and transcended it, which is one of the true measures of leadership.

What seems so compelling about the story of the Constitutional Convention is how current it still sounds. Why? Because the critical elements of human nature, power, and organizations don't change. Human beings are still the same species. A person slapped across the face physically or emotionally still hurts. A failing system still produces fear and the tendency to tear itself apart. Convincing people to operate in their enlightened self-interest can still be a herculean task, because anger, greed, distrust, and the need for status (among other motivations) interfere with their good judgment. Few people wish to give up privilege or autonomy "to promote the general welfare," today or two hundred years ago. And yet somehow, sometimes, a miracle happens. The whole becomes equal to more than the sum of its parts. People and organizations transcend what appear to be impossible forces resisting what must be accomplished for the common good.

## Characteristics of Effective Organizations

In no way do we suggest that the federal system provides an organizational model for any major corporation. Government is government. The goals and methods of government don't work in business and nothing in this section implies otherwise. Although organizations are discussing organizational democracy, it would be suicidal to interpret this as governmental democracy. Rather, the example described above was chosen simply because it is about a time so different and an organization so different. Universal truths should apply to any organization at any time. People are people, and power is power. If we have something to say that is essential, it should apply to any time and any organizational problem.

Nevertheless, the Founding Fathers did create an instrument of republican government unequaled for its longevity, resiliency, and success. One of the reasons is that it embodies a number of characteristics that lie at the foundation of every effective organization:

▲ *Vision-directed.* Out of the intense debates of the convention as well as the long-winded rhetoric of some of the delegates came a clear vision of what the Constitution was intended to accomplish. It is succinctly stated in the Preamble:

> We the People of the United States, in Order to form a more perfect Union, establish Justice, insure domestic Tranquility, provide for the common defense, promote the general Welfare, and secure the Blessings of Liberty to ourselves and our Pos-

terity, do ordain and establish this Constitution for the United States of America.

▲ *Innovative.* We live in an age when organizations like to take great pride in their ability to adapt to change and pioneer innovation. During the eighteenth century, however, innovation was suspect. One contemporary of the Constitution wrote that he didn't think "much good could come of it," because the American people didn't seem "ripe for any great innovations." Nevertheless, the Constitution that the Founding Fathers produced was profoundly innovative. It was evident to all of them that America was different and needed a different form of government. What they created was a republican government, part federal, part national, and completely new.

▲ *Flexible/adaptive.* The Founding Fathers tried to ensure that the Constitution would not be a brittle document that might become outmoded after several decades and fall victim to the type of revolution that had established the American republic in the first place.

▲ *Customer-driven.* Years ago, management gurus began to warn American companies that they had become arrogant and self-satisfied, focused on giving the customers only what the companies wanted and losing sight of what the customers' needs actually were. The result was that major corporations like the automobile manufacturers lost market share to foreign competitors, at least until they eventually got religion and began to preach the gospel of satisfying the customer.

It doesn't take a genius, of course, to know that organizations cannot survive without listening to their customers. The astounding thing is that it took American companies so long to recognize something that the Founding Fathers understood from the very beginning. The American electoral system, federal-state power sharing, and an independent judiciary are all attempts at making our form of government constituent-focused. Unfortunately, during the twentieth century, the exploding size of government bureaucracy and the immense power of special interest groups often seem to prevent the will of the customers from being heard.

## The Heart of the Matter: The Four Levers

How did the Founding Fathers create a government that has so many of the hallmarks of successful organizations? The debates that embroiled the delegates at the Constitutional Convention during those long summer months of 1787 reveal a clear-eyed understanding of the key issues that lie at the center of not only every political institution but, indeed, every organization that is made up of human beings. The solutions are the solutions—they are always the same. Although the words change, the issues don't. Organizations must adapt and innovate as new situations arise; they must motivate their employees; they must serve their customers to survive.

## The Reality of Power

The delegates, we should remember, were practical politicians, not academics, and they based their deliberations on experience, not political theories. General George Washington, for example, was among those who believed that the Articles of Confederation had given too little power to the central government while conceding too much to the individual states. As a result, the states were like a group of planets without a sun—flying off in different directions with no common purpose, no loyalty to the center, no alignment with the goals of the central government. Clearly the federal government needed more power in order to develop common policies in areas such as foreign affairs, trade, and taxes. But how much power? And how much should still remain in the hands of the individual states so that they could respond to problems within their own borders and deal effectively with local problems?

These are the same questions that many organizations face today as they seek to flatten their hierarchies, decentralize their operations, and empower new entities, such as self-directed work teams. How much power should be invested in these teams so that they can respond rapidly to requests from customers or problems on the manufacturing floor? What's to prevent these teams from becoming new power centers that jealously guard their prerogatives and work at cross-purposes, just as the states did in America during the eighteenth century? How do we keep these entities aligned with the common goals of the entire organization so that it can pursue a consistent, successful course of action?

## Human Nature

At the Constitutional Convention, a great deal of time was consumed by a debate over the shape of a new electoral system—whether individual voters should directly elect representatives, senators, and the president. But the real question involved here was not national elections, it was something much broader: *human nature*. How much power should be placed in the hands of the people, and could they be trusted with it?

John Adams, who did not attend the convention but took a keen interest in it from his post as ambassador to England, believed that every person in power was a "ravenous beast of prey" who must be tightly controlled. Some of the delegates agreed with him. James Madison, for example, believed in a government based on the consent of the governed, but he was fearful lest ordinary people have too much involvement and overwhelm the interests of the wealthy. On the other hand, there were many delegates, such as old Benjamin Franklin, who trusted the average citizen far more than the well-to-do. And George Mason from Virginia believed firmly that the people were the only ones to be entrusted with the election of their representatives, although he admitted that some elections might be undermined by graft and corruption.

The Constitutional Convention is a classic example of a successful effort to manage change, and right at the center of it is a discussion of human nature. Perhaps human nature also belongs at the center of deliberations in every modern organization that is considering the change process. How can any company contemplate programs on employee empowerment, team building, reengineering, or total quality management (TQM) without asking itself: What response should we expect from the human beings who work in our organization? How will they deal with the natural anxiety created by change, the confusion, the loss of the familiar? How successful will they be at embracing new cultural values, or developing the new intellectual constructs that change requires?

How will those who have been empowered handle the power and authority that have been given to them? How will the managers and supervisors whose power has been correspondingly diminished react to their new roles in the organization? How will it affect their feelings of self-esteem? their relationships with other employees? their productivity?

The answers, of course, will vary, and they can be hotly debated. But if human nature is not carefully considered—and, unfortunately, many organizations fail to consider it very thoroughly—then the planning and implementation of the change effort may be unrealistic, the responses of employees will seem totally unexpected, and no one may know how to deal with these reactions until it is too late. As a result, the change effort may ultimately fail. Reengineering guru Michael Hammer admits that resistance to change is "natural and inevitable." Why, then, do so many organizations seem totally unprepared to handle it when it arises?

## Role of Leadership

A third issue that confronted the Constitutional Convention was the *role of leadership*. While many of the delegates recognized the need for a strong chief executive (indeed, the absence of one was a major weakness in the Articles of Confederation), they were also profoundly skeptical of their fellow human beings, especially when endowed with considerable power. So they spent many hours debating the role of the president and the powers that should be granted to the presidential office to carry out that role.

Today, the function of leadership continues to be a primary concern of every major organization, many of which spend vast sums of money training executives to become effective leaders. Unfortunately, too many management experts have focused primarily on a leader's style: articulating a vision, using cultural symbols, demonstrating a high level of energy, etc. But leadership is far more than style, as we shall see later in this book.

The essence of successful leadership is knowing how to use power effectively. As Lee Bolman and Terrence Deal point out in their book *Reframing Organizations: Artistry, Choice and Leadership,* effective leaders recognize that the goals and policies of an organization emerge from an ongoing process of bargaining and negotiating among major interest groups who have enduring differences in their perspectives, values, and perceptions. The more diverse the employees and the scarcer the resources, the more horse trading will be necessary. Therefore, a leader must possess the ability to build networks and alliances within a company to get things accomplished, without creating resistance that might derail an entire change effort.

Another essential attribute of leadership is the ability to make sense of the essential dilemmas that lie at the center of any organization: the need for employee empowerment vs. alignment with the overarching goals of the company, to cite just one example. Unless forces such as these are kept in balance, they can disrupt the very fabric of any enterprise.

## Social Process

Perhaps most importantly, a leader must also have an understanding of the *social process* that lies at the center of human organizations and know how to intervene when that process is not working efficiently. A dynamic social process is under way within every corporate enterprise—a clash among various factions, departments, divisions; a struggle between those who perceive themselves as the Outs against those who are seen as the Ins; shifting alliances and conflicts between powerful executives.

The Constitutional Convention was no different. There was a power struggle between the large states, which wanted to control the new government, and the smaller ones, which feared that their interests would be disregarded; leadership within the Convention seemed to shift from week to week among various individuals and factions; there were delegates who tried to dominate and steamroller the proceedings, and others who sat by and said virtually nothing during all the months of debate.

What ultimately saved the Convention was a fortunate combination of factors: a shared vision among the majority of the delegates; the presence of highly respected leaders such as George Washington and Benjamin Franklin; an uncanny understanding of human nature based on the experience gained from practical politics; and, perhaps most significantly, a series of compromises between the delegates over power—power sharing between the states and the federal government, a system of checks and balances within the federal government, and finally the so-called Great Compromise between the smaller and larger states that invested proportional representation in the House of Representatives and equal representation for the states in the Senate.

Vision, leadership, human nature, and power are elements of a complex social process that operates within every organization, not just the political institutions created by the Constitution. No one who contemplates change can expect to be successful without taking these realities into consideration at every stage of the change effort, especially given the unsettled environment in which modern organizations must do business.

## A Turbulent Environment

"It used to be a lot of fun to work ten years ago," confessed the CEO of a *Fortune* 200 company. "You could almost cope. Today, it's almost impossible to cope because things happen at such a rapid rate."

Many top managers might agree with this CEO. Change does seem to be occurring more and more rapidly than ever before, with many diverse forces coming together to create an extremely turbulent business environment. And it is sometimes tempting to look back nostalgically to an earlier era, when doing business was supposedly much easier. Yet, as Robert G. Eccles and Nitin Nohria point out in their book *Beyond the Hype: Rediscovering the Essence of Management,* corporations in the past were dealing with many of the same issues that confront them today. There was anxiety among business leaders over their ability to deal with the increasing rate of technological change, and managerial experts were advising their clients to flatten company hierarchies, driving decision making down to lower levels in order to respond more effectively to customer demands.

Eccles and Nohria quote General Electric president Ralph J. Cordiner as saying in the 1950s that corporations could not "expect to survive without a dynamic plan for continuous innovation" in response to the uncertainties of the changing business landscape.

While some issues never seem to go away, nevertheless today's turbulent environment is distinctly different from anything confronting managers several decades ago. In the generation following World War II, American corporations dominated the globe with little to fear from foreign competitors, who were too busy recovering from the war's devastation. We will never see those days again. Today international competition is a fact of life, and companies that are not prepared to do battle on the world stage may be doomed to disappear from it. When Jack Welch ran GE Plastics in Pittsfield, Massachusetts, he realized that the only way to undercut competitors who were challenging his home markets was to take the struggle to their own turf, which meant taking Plastics global.

Since becoming CEO of GE, one of Welch's many transformations has been making the company, which had been focused almost exclusively on domestic markets, into an international giant. Today GE revenues coming from abroad are substantially higher than what they were ten years ago. Through joint ventures with overseas concerns or by starting new businesses, GE has rapidly expanded its reach into Asia and Latin America—areas of the world where, Welch recognizes, the company must compete if it is to prosper.

## Information

Another key area where today's business environment has changed is information technology. In corporate hierarchies, executives at the top of the pyramid used to have an iron grip on the flow of information, and they determined who had access to it. Now, with computer networks, virtually every employee has access to the same information, enabling them to perform an end run around the hierarchy—one reason why the old corporate structures seem to have become obsolete.

The rapid flow of information across national boundaries is also compelling companies to become global, just as GE has done. Indeed, information, as Peter Drucker points out, may be the most important business resource. "If you apply knowledge to existing products or services, you achieve productivity," Drucker adds. "If you apply knowledge to new products and services, you achieve innovation. Organizations will need to learn to work simultaneously on innovation and productivity."

Unfortunately, it's simply not enough for a company to come up with innovative ideas; it must also bring them to the marketplace rapidly. One of the reasons that large companies, such as DuPont, have reduced layers of hierarchy is that decisions were being made far too slowly, making it impossible to compete with smaller firms that could develop products faster and make them available to customers much sooner. Continuous downsizing has improved the ability of the giants like DuPont to innovate and market new products, to say nothing of what it's done for the bottom line. But in the process, downsizing has also changed the life of every employee.

The old contract of a lifetime job from the company for a lifetime of loyalty from its employees has been irrevocably shattered. Unfortunately, nothing has arisen to take its place. Today, each employee realizes that the first commitment must be to self. The employee must take advantage of any opportunity offered by an employer to broaden skills so that he or she can then shop them somewhere else. Paradoxically, the only security may be in constant change: moving from job to job, constantly improving your résumé, so that you're never caught in a job that is being eliminated or with an expertise that has become obsolete. But where does this leave the organization? Without the long-term loyalty of its employees, how can it function effectively? What new contract will replace the old one?

## Twelve Hallmarks of Success

Companies that wish to compete successfully in a turbulent business environment characterized by global competition, exploding information technology, fast-paced change, and new employer-employee relationships will inevitably be forced to make significant adjustments in the way they operate. From interviews with more than 1,000 senior executives and academics, experts at the University of Pennsylvania's Wharton School have developed a set of twelve hallmarks that will characterize the leading corporations of the twenty-first century:

1. *Vision-directed.* This means having a statement of principles that is not just some high-sounding words tacked up on the wall of the company cafeteria, but a rather clear set of values that actually influence a company's operations and give employees a strong sense of pride in their organization. Levi Strauss, for example, removed $40 million worth of business from China and took similar action in Myanmar (Burma) in protest over human rights violations by these totalitarian regimes. In addition, according to *Business Week*, when Levi Strauss discovered that two of its contractors in Bangladesh were employing underage children in their factories, the company forced this practice to stop. Then, after being informed that these boys and girls were the sole support of their families, Levi Strauss not only persuaded the contractors to continue paying them, but itself sent the children back to school and shouldered the entire cost until they were old enough to return to work. That's putting your money where your principles are.

2. *Cross-functional.* Asea Brown Boveri is a giant corporation with tens of thousands of employees doing business in hundreds of local companies located across the globe. ABB cannot afford to be organized along traditional functional lines (e.g., marketing, manufacturing, R&D) because business decisions involve continuous coordination among many functions.

Instead, ABB has a matrix organizational structure, with its local companies grouped by products and services, and again by geographical location. Rubbermaid, the innovative manufacturer of plastic products, relies on cross-functional business teams to come up with new ideas and carry them through each stage of development. These teams give employees a sense of ownership of the product and a commitment to its success.

3. *Flatter and empowered.* Information technology, intense competition, and the rapid rate of change have made the old, rigid hierarchies obsolete. Decision making simply cannot move up and down the corporate silos fast enough, so organizations must be flattened and individuals at every level must be empowered to make decisions. But, as John Kotter argues in *The Leadership Factor,* this requires more from managers than they were ever asked to do before. "Figuring out the right thing to do in an environment of uncertainty . . . and then getting others to accept a new way of doing things demand skills and approaches that most managers did not need in the past. It demands more than technical expertise, administrative ability, and traditional management. Operating in the new environment also requires leadership." So an effort at developing leaders throughout the organization must accompany efforts at empowerment and flattening the corporate hierarchy.

4. *Global.* Companies like Ford have recognized the advantages that globalization can mean, from buying materials and services in low-cost areas of the world to developing new markets that can help cushion the blow when your domestic sales take a downturn.

5. *Networked.* Instead of carrying out every function on their own, companies will often find it far more cost-effective to create partnering arrangements with other firms to perform certain functions. Outsourcing, for example, is currently occurring in the banking field, where one major bank recently hired outside vendors for its legal, audit, and cafeteria operations.

6. *Information-technology–based.* Computers and communication systems will continue to alter the way companies operate internally while improving relationships with suppliers and customers. At large law firms, for example, computer networks now enable corporate clients to regularly review the work the firm is currently performing on their cases as well as the number of hours being billed to each case.

7. *Stakeholder-focused.* As Dr. Jerry Wind of the Wharton School explains, "A company will not be able to operate as a closed entity cut off from society's needs and demands. Management will still give primary attention to its shareholders, . . . [but] increasingly, governments, environmental organizations, ethnic and minority groups, and other bodies will hold firms accountable for their actions." An excellent example is the Chemical Manufacturing Association, whose member companies have developed a far-reaching initiative called Responsible Care. As part of Responsible Care, chemical companies include ordinary citizens on plant advisory panels and keep them informed of the facility's operations; they hold open houses to explain chemical manufacturing processes and attempt to allay any fears expressed by the community; and they sponsor joint safety drills with community fire departments and emergency medical teams so that everyone will be prepared in case of a chemical emergency.

8. *Flexible/adaptive.* One of the best predictors of a company's long-term performance is its ability to adapt to changes in the marketplace. This requires a culture that encourages experimentation and intelligent risk taking, that incorporates new ideas into the fabric of its operations, and that provides employees with abundant opportunities to develop new skills so that they can keep pace with change. At Motorola, for example, the emphasis is on lifelong learning, with employees attending more hours of training annually than at almost any other company in America. Training programs have enabled the company to achieve an exceptional reputation for product quality and maintain positions of leadership in areas such as computer chips, cellular telephones, and paging equipment.

9. *Customer-driven.* While many companies talk about getting close to the customer, some are actually trying to achieve it. Weyerhauser, according to *Fortune*, recognizes that the best way for manufacturing employees to understand customers' needs to regularly travel to their facilities and find out firsthand how they use Weyerhauser products. The result: significant product improvements.

10. *Total quality–focused.* If any single element can be called the foundation stone of the change process, it is the emphasis on quality. After World War II, W. Edwards Deming and Joseph Juran taught the Japanese the importance of quality and how to attain it. Eventually American companies got the quality religion and began singing out of the same hymnbook, just in time to win back some of their customers from the Japanese. Some of these companies (e.g., Motorola and Federal Express) have even been recognized for their efforts by receiving the prestigious Malcolm Baldrige National Quality Award.

11. *Time-based.* Developing a new product rapidly and bringing it to the marketplace ahead of the competition can spell the difference between a company's success or failure. In his book *What America Does Right,* Robert Waterman describes Procter & Gamble's plant in Lima, Ohio, which was given the job of manufacturing the company's improved Downy fabric softener. Lima succeeded in overhauling its production equipment so rapidly that new Downy was rolling off the assembly line and into supermarkets in the unbelievable time of only sixteen weeks. The key, according to Waterman, was the plant's empowered work teams that took ownership for the project and held a large stake in its success.

12. *Innovative. Innovative* and *entrepreneurial* are words most of us associate with small or medium-sized companies. Yet some of the large corporations—the elephants—have also learned how to run with the gazelles. Through a variety of methods, companies like General Electric, Motorola, Federal Express, and P&G have proved that they can compete successfully. Unfortunately, too many other U.S. companies are still struggling to find a change process that will make them more competitive.

## Carrying Out a Change Process

With the information gathered from so many senior executives, we now have a consensus on what needs to happen in an organization—the twelve hallmarks—if it is to be successful. What we lack is a clear understanding of *how* to make these changes occur. The two most common misconceptions about how to carry out a change process are, on the one hand, that it must be directed from the top, and on the other hand, that people must be brought together to discuss it. Both have proved over time to be largely ineffective in dealing with organizational problems.

The CEO of a worldwide organization told us how angry he was when, after ordering that the name of his company be changed, he would drive by manufacturing plants and notice that the signs standing out in front of them still bore the company's old name. Organizational theory holds that the simpler and clearer the task, the easier it is to direct from above. What could be easier than ordering sign changes? Yet nothing happened. Why not?

Some management experts might believe that the CEO had not consulted enough of his subordinates in making the decision. Therefore, they simply decided not to implement it. And yet, when organizations empower groups at all levels to sit down and make every small decision, what usually happens if they can't agree? Organizational paralysis—a pitfall that is often a result of participative management. Would participative management really have solved the CEO's problem with the signs? Before we can answer that, we must understand why people were so resistant to changing them. Then it might be possible to figure out how to defuse their resistance. For our CEO, this might require a keener understanding of the subtleties of human nature, how to use power adroitly without creating a backlash, and how to build a consensus to support the sign change.

If the simple process of changing a sign is difficult, just imagine how much harder it is to adopt one of the twelve hallmarks, such as becoming total quality–focused or customer-driven. What's more, it's not enough to adopt one of these hallmarks; a company usually must attack a number of different areas simultaneously. Improving customer focus, for instance, may also mean that an organization must become more flexible and adaptive, flatter and more empowered, more innovative, and more information-driven.

Management consultants have largely been acting as if there is a single ball and they know how to get it moving and direct it. This has led many companies to opt for the quick fix, the silver bullet, that they think will make the change process easier: downsizing, restructuring, reengineering, self-directed work teams, stripping away layers of hierarchy. One company we know has tried all of these approaches, one after the other, and so far the culture has proved completely resistant to full-scale change (human nature often seems to react this way). The only result has been to produce thousands of cynical employees—in-house skeptics who have lost faith in their organization or the intelligence of its management. They shake their heads wearily as each new consultant enters the stately confines of company headquarters with his or her particular brand of change. One of the latest efforts, begun some years ago, was TQM, which met the same fate as every process that had gone before it. "It was the most ridiculous thing I ever heard of," one employee told us. "It cost millions of dollars and we didn't get anything for it."

Similar comments can be heard in scores of other organizations where employees have been worn out by the "flavor of the month" panacea. Frequently, the problem is that these so-called silver bullets focus on only one of the twelve hallmarks, such as quality improvement. The others receive scant attention or are completely overlooked, until someone realizes how closely they are interrelated. By that time, momentum may be carrying the organization in the wrong direction. Making a midcourse correction is similar to changing the direction of a giant ball that is rolling downhill. Instead of doing this, the change effort is abandoned—at least, until another panacea is proposed and the organization takes off in a different direction. Meanwhile employees are growing more disillusioned and disgruntled and increasingly resistant to change. How can this resistance be overcome? Often the answer is by utilizing the levers of corporate change.

# 2

# Change Begins: Does It Always Take a Crisis?

In the spring of 1862, the Confederate States of America faced the gravest crisis in its brief and turbulent history. What had begun so gloriously with the victory at Fort Sumter only a year earlier, followed closely by the great triumph on the dusty battlefield of Manassas, now seemed to have turned to ashes. In April, the southern jewel of New Orleans had fallen to a northern flotilla commanded by the redoubtable David Farragut. And only a few weeks earlier, General Ulysses S. Grant had beaten back a determined Confederate attack at Shiloh, in the process killing the South's most renowned general, Albert Sidney Johnston.

Now another Johnston, Joseph Eggleston, faced an overwhelming federal invasion force on the peninsula between the York and James rivers, a mighty army of 100,000 that was inexorably bearing down on the Confederate capital. So far the only strategy that Johnston had been able to devise to deal with this threat to the South's jugular was a series of strategic retreats, much to the consternation of his commander-in-chief, Jefferson Davis, president of the Confederacy. Davis was even more frustrated by Johnston's infuriating habit of never explaining his battle plans. To the highly sensitive president, who regarded himself as a talented military strategist, this seemed like a calculated insult. After graduating from West Point, Davis had fought with distinction in the Mexican War, and later served as secretary of war in the administration of President James Buchanan just before the outbreak of the current hostilities.

It was, therefore, a highly charged atmosphere that surrounded the Executive Mansion in Richmond when Johnston was summoned to attend a meeting with Davis and his military adviser, Robert E. Lee. Both men pressed the proud, testy commanding general to make a stand at York-town and stop the Federals before they could advance any closer to Richmond, but he refused to listen to them. Fortunately, in George Brinton McClellan, Johnston faced a Union commander even more cautious than he was. While the Confederate forces facing him were only half the size of his own army, McClellan was convinced that Johnston possessed double his numbers. And the Union spy chief, Allen Pinkerton, kept providing McClellan with information that only confirmed his worst fears. As a result, "Little Mac" inched his way forward, laying siege to Yorktown, then gradually advancing westward to Williamsburg, the old colonial capital. Meanwhile, his relations with his own commander-in-chief, Abraham Lincoln, were if anything even worse than those between Davis and the secretive Johnston. McClellan regarded the president as an ignorant baboon, and Lincoln, in turn, accused his general of suffering from a terminal case of "the slows."

But "the slows" might just prove to be good enough. As the days of May grew longer and hotter, McClellan's grand army drew to within three miles of Richmond, so close that Union soldiers could hear the city's church bells ringing. President Davis had already sent his wife and children south to North Carolina, and the Confederate Congress had abruptly adjourned, its members scurrying for safety to their far-flung homes. "The Enemy are at the gates. Who will take the lead and act, act, act?" asked the *Richmond Dispatch.*

Finally, during the last days of May, Johnston turned and fell upon the Federals. But the Battle of Fair Oaks, as it was called, proved inconclusive. Johnston's field commanders (who according to some reports spent as much time bickering among themselves as they did fighting the enemy) seemed unable to coordinate their attacks into anything that even faintly resembled a well-timed operation. Perhaps the only fortunate event to occur at the battle was that Johnston himself was seriously wounded in the right shoulder, knocking him out of action for the immediate future. As he joined the flood of Confederate casualties streaming into Richmond's hospitals, the Federal soldiers seemed poised to overrun the capital. "No city in the world was sadder than Richmond in those days," a Confederate private wrote.

President Davis faced a critical decision. He could replace Johnston with one of the battle-hardened commanders of the Army of Northern Virginia or send for one of his generals from the western theater. But Davis did neither. Instead, he appointed a man with almost no leadership experience on the battlefield: his military adviser, Robert E. Lee. It would prove the best decision the president made during his entire term in office.

At first, Lee's appointment met with considerable skepticism from the men under his command. What could so untested a general know about defeating such a formidable opponent, they wondered. But it had been Lee who insisted on reinforcing Stonewall Jackson in the Shenandoah Valley, where he brilliantly outmaneuvered three Union armies and threatened Washington, thus preventing Lincoln from sending McClellan the reinforcements that might have put just enough backbone into him to risk attacking Richmond. And it was Lee who also recognized that in the end even the cautious McClellan would be victorious if the South remained on the defensive.

Leaving the terrain directly in front of the capital only lightly defended, Lee divided his forces and prepared a massive assault on McClellan's flank. It was an incredible risk—but Lee would take such risks again and again as the war progressed, earning a reputation as one of the great riverboat gamblers of military history. The fact was that Lee had little choice; what's more, the dire circumstances in which he found himself gave the Confederate commander an opportunity to catch the enemy off balance and perhaps defeat him.

Ordering Jackson back from the valley, Lee struck first at Mechanicsville in late June 1862. Although the bloody contest was far from a decisive victory, it proved enough to frighten the timid McClellan into beginning his retreat from Richmond. In a weeklong series of engagements, Lee hammered the Union army repeatedly, his intent being not just to push McClellan eastward but to crush his entire force.

As it turned out, poor staff work and inept communication between Lee and his subordinates prevented the Confederate commander from realizing his goal. Lee and his generals were as yet not fully experienced in directing so large an army and leading it to decisive victory. That would come later. Nevertheless, Richmond had been saved. And Jefferson Davis, after taking a considerable gamble, had finally found someone to whom he could entrust the Confederacy's fortunes. Not only could Lee win, he also knew enough to keep Davis informed of his battle plans. It would prove to be one of those rare marriages between military and political leaders that worked, and it would enable the South to remain in the war for three more years.

## The Impact of Crisis

A chronicle of the events of 1862 is a study in crisis—a crisis that led to the selection of a new leader who changed the direction of an organization. Lee's appointment also ended a power struggle between the president and his commanding general and eventually improved the alignment of the Confederacy's subordinate generals with their commander, which helped bring the Army of Northern Virginia enormous success on the battlefield. In most organizations, crisis often seems to be the necessary catalyst for large-scale change. Suddenly alternatives that seemed unthinkable only a short time earlier appear eminently practical. The specter of impending disaster shifts all the parameters and forces people into a "let's try anything" mentality, which is frequently the necessary prerequisite for change.

Upon assuming office in 1933, Franklin Roosevelt said, "America wants action, action now." And that's what he began to give the nation with a series of experimental programs known collectively as the New Deal. The crisis of the Great Depression enabled the federal government to suddenly begin playing a role that would have seemed unimaginable only a few years earlier. The reason, of course, was that all the ground rules had suddenly changed. Millions of middle-class Americans who had grown up believing that their willingness to work would always guarantee them a job now found themselves standing in unemployment lines. They wanted someone to help them, and the New Dealers tried to do just that.

While the American experience during the Great Depression is in no way meant as a blueprint for business organizations, it does, nevertheless, point up the way in which severe crisis can produce enormous change. Several decades later, U.S. automobile manufacturers faced a crisis of sharply declining markets during the 1980s and responded with quality programs, teamwork between managers and employees, and an increased attention to customer demands—changes that would have seemed impossible previously. Similar stories can, of course, be told in many other major American industries, from computers and steel manufacturing to hotel chains and health care.

## A Catalyst for New Leadership

In many organizations, a crisis frequently brings in new leadership. Indeed, if you're looking for a sure sign that the old order has been discredited, just keep your eye on the large corner office. At one Eastern bank, for example, that office had been specially fitted with a revolving door, through which three CEOs came and went in a little over five years. Each was sure that he held the key to making the bank more competitive, and each proved to be no more successful than his predecessor. A new leader, Robert E. Lee to the contrary, will not always help an organization in crisis; he or she must take the organization in the right direction.

The first CEO, who had been a senior vice president for finance, concentrated on cost-cutting measures—closing branches and laying off personnel. While this seemed a logical course to follow, in reality it was completely counterproductive. The new CEO had failed to define the bank's primary niche in the marketplace, which was serving consumers. His cost cutting simply succeeded in undermining this effort, while at the same time demoralizing many of the bank's employees, who found themselves stretched too thin to serve their customers effectively.

Following the CEO's abrupt departure, the bank brought in a change agent who had turned around another financial services company. His vision was to create a big bank that would dominate the region, and so he immediately embarked on an acquisition spree. For a short period, everyone became caught up in the momentum: The bank was becoming larger, and that, in itself, seemed like a positive direction. Unfortunately, this CEO did not define the bank's niche any better than the previous one had. There was no guiding plan behind the bank's acquisitions, nor did it possess enough administrative talent to successfully incorporate them into its existing structure. As a result, the bank simply increased its debt load without improving its competitive position.

The third CEO to occupy the corner office was the only one who clearly recognized that the bank had to focus on the consumer marketplace. By this time, however, it was almost too late to make any difference. Employees had suffered enough, and they seemed thoroughly demoralized. Nevertheless, the new CEO decided to call in a highly touted marketing consultant, whose inspirational approach actually succeeded in energizing the bank's tellers and other employees who dealt directly with the customer. For several months, they brought a higher level of enthusiasm to their jobs. But it didn't last. The employees gradually realized that when they tried to carry out the CEO's vision, they were being stonewalled by several layers of middle managers who felt uncomfortable with the bank's new approach to customer service.

## The Human Reaction to Change

The reaction of these middle managers is fairly typical of people who are confronted with change. Although they seemed to buy into the CEO's new vision, they didn't really understand it. And even if they had understood it, most of them lacked the skills to carry it out. Those few that did could not count on their fellow managers having these skills. And it doesn't take too many unskilled people at critical points to make a new vision unworkable.

The change effort must have seemed very unsettling to these managers, who probably believed that it would fail just like its predecessors. Perhaps they felt as if the CEO was asking them to head off on a journey into the unknown, like astronauts landing on a distant planet, without any of the tools to achieve success. Under the most ideal conditions (which hardly existed at the bank), such a change can produce enormous anxiety. Suddenly the managers were expected to operate in a new environment and perform their jobs differently. This is enough to make anyone feel insecure and fearful of failure. And any manager would surely see the possibility of failure as a threat to his or her position in the bank.

The CEO had failed to recognize these salient realities of human nature. He had also overlooked the importance of achieving alignment and support from his subordinates before embarking on a new course. These mistakes, sadly, proved to be his undoing.

## More Than a Crisis

While a crisis may be enough to initiate a change process, it takes far more to make that process work. The leader must also have an effective strategy for transforming the organization. This does not just mean a broad knowledge of the marketplace and how to compete in it, and what internal structures must be put in place to make the company successful. It also involves an understanding of the human beings in the organization—how they will react to the change effort and how to ensure that they will give it their support.

### Crisis at an HMO

Several years ago a health maintenance organization (HMO) was experiencing serious financial problems. A series of factors had led to the HMO's current fiscal crisis.

First, new members were not being enrolled in large enough numbers to make the HMO solidly profitable. Indeed, some members had even begun dropping out because of poor service. Second, the number of bed days in the hospital for each thousand patients—a critical measure of an HMO's financial stability because hospital stays are so expensive—was more than three times the average. Third, although it wished to employ all its own physicians, the HMO was too small to cover every medical specialty, and so it had to contract for some of them. However, these costs had ballooned out of control. Finally, administrative costs had also risen excessively, further exacerbating the organization's precarious financial situation. Indeed, on its present course, the HMO would become financially insolvent within three to four months.

While these were the immediate factors behind the HMO's financial problems, the underlying cause was a power struggle between the physicians and the administration. The animosity between these two factions

## Figure 2-1. Structure of the HMO.

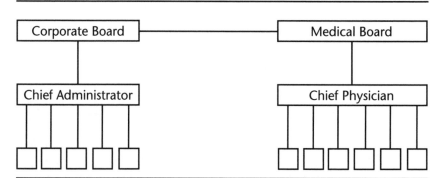

permeated every level of the organization. Indeed, at the HMO's individual clinics, secretaries, billing clerks, and other members of the administration were barely on speaking terms with the physicians. So severe was the resentment between them that it could not always be successfully concealed from the patients, in some cases significantly affecting the service they received and even causing them to disenroll from the HMO.

The men who led each faction within the organization seemed powerless to improve things. The head physician, for example, was a middle-aged internist, beloved by his subordinates but with almost no managerial ability. He reported to a board of his fellow physicians, who dictated policy to him and expected him to carry their demands to the administration and secure approval for everything the doctors wanted. The chief administrator, a CPA, could best be described as conflict-avoidant. Not only did he shrink from any confrontations with the doctors, he was also ill equipped to resolve any of the problems besetting his own administrative departments. The result was a stalemate that produced a rapidly worsening situation for the HMO.

### Problems of Personalities, Loyalties, Time, and Money

There's a saying that "the seed of the solution is always present in the problem; its advantages are just misunderstood." Let's see how the crisis was effectively utilized to help the HMO. The structure of the HMO is shown in Figure 2-1. It had both an administrative and a physician organization, with no one having the ultimate authority to bring both sides together.

A different structure by itself, however, would not have been sufficient to solve the problem. Let's suppose that the physicians reported to the administrators and the chief administrator had the power to fire the

**Figure 2-2. Another possible structure for the HMO.**

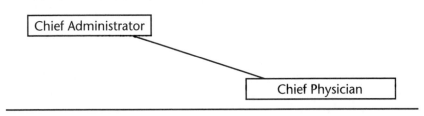

chief physician. (See Figure 2-2.) What would happen? The head physician's position would become vacant. Unfortunately, the chief administrator didn't have the skills to do this job, and he was already so overworked that if he had tried, this would only have distracted him further from other critical tasks, such as directing the sales force. Also, the doctors and other medical personnel were very loyal to the chief physician. The shock and hostility caused by his firing would more than likely make the clinical departments even more resistant to change and more alienated from the head of the HMO. Third, since the organization had only enough money remaining to survive for an additional three to four months, there wasn't time to fire one chief physician and hire another.

### Change Resulting From the Crisis

The key to this situation did not lie in the structure of the organization, or in firing the chief physician, but in the fact that the organization was failing. While at first that might appear to be an insurmountable problem, it could also serve as an enormous lever for change. Most people have a strong desire to see their organization survive. If it doesn't, they will lose their jobs, which may prove difficult to replace. Also, employees who work together day after day for several years develop a strong sense of identity and purpose that is closely tied to the success of what they are doing. No one wants to be associated with a failing organization. But this can be a double-edged sword. On the one hand, it can galvanize individuals to deal with the problems in their organization. On the other hand, it might persuade them to completely disassociate themselves from it. Think of any voluntary organization of which you are or have been a member. It could be a church, a social club, a sports team, or a professional group. Suppose that each time you showed up, there were fewer people present than at the previous meeting. How would you feel? How would you like to attend a meeting and find yourself the only person there?

Sometimes the wish to avoid this type of feeling, coupled with realistic concerns about a job and future income, can accelerate the demise of an organization. Belief and perception are powerful and often self-confirming. Once the members of an organization sense its failure, they may withdraw their investment in it and flee, thus creating the very outcome they feared. Emotion largely directs human motivation. Few managers any longer believe in the "rational model of human beings"—that employees leave (or should leave) their emotions at the door of their companies. Greed, jealousy, and envy . . . excitement, loss, and hurt . . . the need to experience feelings of achievement, importance, and security—these are some of the powerful emotional factors that motivate human behavior.

As we shall see, the initiation of change is also an emotional process, not a rational one. That's why a crisis can work for or against an organization. It can inspire employees to pull together and help their organization survive, or it can convince them to withdraw and flee. Therefore, confronting employees with the fact that the HMO they work for will go broke by the end of the next quarter is a high-risk strategy. However, unless some large lever like a crisis is used, the organization will fail anyway. One advantage of real crises is that they often turn a high-risk strategy into a lower-risk one.

What are the key factors to consider when you decide whether to take advantage of a crisis?

1. It must be perceived by employees as clear and irrefutable. If there is too much doubt about the reality of the crisis, a significant number of employees will feel manipulated and attack top management, weakening the organization even further.

2. The time frame is important. The crisis must be perceived as urgent enough to stimulate employees to immediate action, but the time frame must be long enough to allow for hope that something positive can be accomplished. If the crisis lasts too long, employees will become exhausted, unable to keep up the effort to produce change. Most people can sprint a few hundred yards, but a marathon will exhaust them. On the other hand, change takes time. If the crisis seems too overwhelming and hopeless, employees will simply give up.

3. The discussion of the crisis cannot be too hot or too cold. If there is too little emotion, employees will not have enough motivation to change their behavior and perception. If there is too much, it will lead employees to blame and attack one another or top management, resulting in too much disruption. Think of a fire in a theater and the panic it produces. The people there are motivated to save themselves, not fix the problem.

4. Employees must clearly perceive that action is possible, and that tasks must be quickly assigned or undertaken by them. It is only as they become involved in fixing the crisis and see the results of their work that their belief in the organization and its leaders will be strengthened.

### Breaking the Deadlock at the HMO

In the case of the HMO, the means chosen to break this deadlock was a workshop for sixty people, thirty physicians and an equal number of administrators, drawn from every level of the HMO. The workshop opened with an audiovisual presentation by the comptroller, whose graphs and charts graphically portrayed that if it continued on its current course, the HMO would cease to operate in three months.

The reaction from the audience was nothing less than stunned silence, for many of them had had absolutely no idea how critical the situation had actually become. By apprising them of the problem and creating an atmosphere of crisis, it was hoped, an opportunity could be found to make the profound and rapid changes that were necessary if the HMO was to be rescued.

Having captured the attention of the audience, the organizers of the meeting next introduced a speaker from one of the country's leading HMOs, who outlined the benchmarks that defined successful organizations in the health maintenance field; these included bed days per thousand, specialist costs, and key service indicators. Once the workshop participants fully understood where their HMO was and where it needed to be, the next task was enabling them to get there.

First, the power struggle that had raged for so long between the physicians and the administrators had to be defused. From conversations with employees on both sides before the workshop, the organizers had developed a clear understanding of the key issues that seemed to divide them. Next, they wanted to give the workshop participants an opportunity to express their feelings regarding these issues, framed in the form of questions. The chance to ventilate usually acts as an icebreaker that unlocks communication, leads to a candid exchange of ideas, and builds support for the change process. However, it would easily take several days for each of sixty people to answer a half dozen different questions. They couldn't spare that much time from their jobs.

So the participants were divided into mixed groups of twelve, with six doctors seated in a line across from six administrators. Each person asked the one sitting across from him or her a question (for example, What do you see as the major reason why we're not growing faster?), then simply recorded the answer for five minutes, without making any attempt to either agree or disagree. Afterward, the roles were reversed.

At the end of a ten-minute session, every individual in the room had begun to ventilate about the problems that were facing him or her. The same procedure was repeated for the other questions. By the time an hour had ended, the sixty people had gotten a lot of pent-up feelings off their chests and had also begun to see problems from the other group's perspective.

This exercise, which is called the *universal solvent*, opens up almost any organization. There is an explosion of communication—you can hear it in the rising decibel level throughout the room. Participants generally experience a feeling of freedom and excitement, for they sense that the deadlock is finally broken.

Following the exercise, the responses to each question were collected, and those voiced most frequently were listed on flip charts. These were the major problems that the HMO had to begin to address. But before starting that process, the participants went through another exercise. Each group (physicians and administrators) was asked to talk separately about how they saw themselves, how they saw the other group, and how they thought the other group saw them. Finally, in thirty one-on-one conversations (one physician and one administrator), the participants talked about the results of these discussions. This exercise further broadened their perspective and deepened their understanding of the other group's point of view.

The groundwork had now been laid for the physicians and administrators to work together on the issues that confronted the entire organization. For too long, each group had been blaming the other for every problem. While this was a convenient way to avoid responsibility, it solved absolutely nothing. Take the problem of enrolling too few new members, for example. In the past, the marketing people had believed that the doctors were driving patients away by giving them poor service, while the doctors had blamed the marketing department for not recruiting enough new members. Since neither side was willing to talk, the problem simply grew worse. Now both sides began to see that they were the cause as well as the solution. And together they began to develop a series of concrete plans to deal with each problem effectively. As a result, the financial health of the HMO improved rapidly, and in a few months it was on the road to a full recovery.

Why had this change process worked? The crisis acted as a catalyst that provided some impetus for change. But by itself that would not have been enough to persuade the physicians and administrators, who were barely on speaking terms, to sit down and begin talking about a strategy to improve their HMO. Nor could a leader have suddenly announced a new vision and direction for the organization and expected everyone to simply sign on and support him or her. For a short time there might have been a willingness among the employees to try something new, but the fact that they didn't know how to cooperate with one another would have rapidly undermined their efforts.

The answer lay, instead, in the principles we discussed earlier. First, the crisis was clearly and carefully documented in the audiovisual presentation delivered by the comptroller. In addition, an expert from a leading HMO demonstrated to the assembled group of employees that their organization was sadly deficient in all the critical benchmarks of success. Second, the three-month window was brief enough to galvanize employees into immediate action, but not so short that the situation appeared hopeless. Third, the training exercises, such as the universal solvent, unleashed enough emotion to motivate employees to change the direction of their organization. Finally, the employees began to plan a series of concrete activities designed to deal with the crisis. Buoyed by the sense that they were finally moving forward, the doctors and administrators aligned themselves behind common goals and carried out improvement programs that saved their struggling organization.

## Change Without a Crisis

Can large-scale organizational change occur without the type of crisis we have described? Sometimes, but it's one of the most difficult and misunderstood adventures possible to undertake. Many such efforts fail utterly, while others achieve only a partial success. To a certain extent, of course, organizations are changing continually. New products are developed, new markets are successfully penetrated, new managers and employees are hired. What we are discussing, however, is far more fundamental. Every so often, a new leader comes to the helm of an organization, and suddenly it seems to burst forth with enormous activity. A company that long seemed stagnant—losing its way in the world of corporate competition, its customers feeling virtually ignored, its employees lacking direction—springs miraculously to life under the guidance of a dynamic leader. Do such leaders possess some mystical gift, or are they operating within the framework of an understandable set of laws?

Management experts have proposed two kinds of change: primary and secondary, also known as fundamental. Primary change is like that on the face of a clock. The hands move around a fixed set of numbers, but nothing ever really changes. Systems often tend to reach equilibrium, with self-reinforcing cycles that keep fundamental change from occurring. For example, in order to show regular growth in profits and revenues and keep its stock price attractive, an organization may continually acquire other companies. Management directs its attention and skills to acquisitions and their successful integration into the parent company. Therefore, the enterprise never develops a sales culture. Unfortunately, the lack of sales threatens to slow revenue growth and profits. But the organization cannot risk taking the necessary time to develop an effective sales function. Instead, it continues to concentrate on more acquisitions.

Suppose a new CEO wants to break this cycle. She might go out and hire an aggressive head of sales with a proven track record, and he might begin to develop a sales organization. But the culture lacks the necessary systems to support such an organization, and the vice president of sales is operating outside the norms of the culture. So there must be a sufficient number of managers who understand what he is trying to do and willingly cooperate with him or his effort will fail. Unfortunately, this process takes time, and there is enormous pressure on the company to achieve rapid and continuous financial growth. So the effort inevitably flounders. Instead of making a fundamental change, the company returns to the old cycle, in which change follows a fixed pattern like the hands of a clock.

Second-order, or fundamental, change is quite different. It alters the entire context. To accomplish such a sweeping goal, four things must happen:

1. The change process must tap into one or more strong emotions. As we said before, it is emotion that largely governs human motivation. For employees to have an intellectual realization that the organization must change is simply not enough to make it happen. They must be motivated by something more: the fear of losing their job, greed for a higher income, the desire for more power, the need to be part of a winning team, a feeling of accomplishment, recognition from top management.

2. The leader must find a way to destabilize the existing system—that is, fundamentally alter the equilibrium that prevents change. The destabilizing process must also be strong enough not to lose momentum, resulting in the system's returning to where it was before, or to an even worse equilibrium. Think of a rocket that is launched into space with too little velocity to go into orbit and crashes to the ground instead. Often the fallout from a change effort that doesn't succeed is worse than not initiating a change effort in the first place. Just ask the employees at many of those organizations that have attempted a succession of panaceas, one after the other, in an effort to transform their operations.

3. The change must be self-reinforcing, propelling the system permanently into a new configuration. In organic chemistry, when crude petroleum at a refinery is broken down, the hydrocarbon molecule goes through a brief transition state called a free radical. If the energy is insufficient, or no catalyst is present, this free radical will not be transformed

into gasoline. However, once it becomes gasoline, it cannot go back to being heavy crude again.

4. There must be a vision or ideology that explains why the change process is occurring in a way that supports the credibility and legitimacy of the organization's leadership. Fundamental change naturally produces anger and anxiety in many employees. Some will resist it because they're anxious about whether they can function in a new environment, they lack confidence in their ability as old dogs to learn new tricks, they're afraid of failure, or they're fearful of what might happen to their jobs if they do fail—to name only a few reasons why they don't rush to embrace change. Others see their power and prestige being undermined—the respect they receive from subordinates, the perks and privileges that they've spent years working to obtain. And it's only natural for them to fight to preserve them.

Somehow these feelings must be defused by a vision that is compelling enough to power the change process. What's also necessary is a dynamic leader with both an impressive track record of past successes that will persuade others to follow him and the grit and determination that it takes to go the distance.

## The General Electric Experience

Let's see how the factors just discussed operated at General Electric after Jack Welch became CEO and engineered perhaps the most celebrated corporate turnaround ever to occur in the absence of an immediate crisis. When Welch took command in 1980, GE appeared to be a highly successful corporation—indeed, one of the most prestigious in the world. But Welch saw what most others seemingly failed to realize: The company wasn't bringing new ideas to the marketplace fast enough, many of its products were too high-priced to remain competitive, productivity was declining, and most of its businesses had barely penetrated the international markets. But how could he convince anyone else of these problems when the company appeared to be so solid? Although he had a highly successful track record and a very forceful personality, these were not enough.

Welch decided to light a fire under GE by initiating a fundamental change process. He began by destabilizing the system. In what has now become a legendary event in the annals of corporate America, he announced that any business that was not number one or number two in terms of market share must achieve this ranking or it would be sold. At first, many of GE's executives simply didn't believe him. But Welch meant exactly what he said, and years of corporate upheaval followed: Tens of thousands of employees were laid off, layers of bureaucracy were eliminated, many businesses were sold off, and decision making was pushed further and further down the corporate ladder, all in an effort to improve productivity and respond to the demands of the customer more rapidly so that GE businesses would be leaders in their respective fields.

In short, what Welch had done was to supply the change initiative with enough energy that it could not crash and burn, returning the company to the old equilibrium. He made it clear that there was no going back.

In the old GE, for example, the head of each business had to submit an elaborate annual strategic plan that required six to eight months of research and analysis. Then the plan had to be approved by the corporate planning staff, a powerful group of naysayers who looked for any reason to shoot down a manager's request. Welch turned this power structure on its head. He transformed the planning staffers into advisers to the business managers, and put strategic planning in the hands of each business. Then he forced the managers to slash costs and rethink their markets.

### A Bumpy Road to Change

GE's bottom line grew stronger, but, as it turned out, this proved to be only half the battle. Morale at the company was sagging. The change process had produced enormous anxiety and uncertainty among the employees. Having grown up in the old GE culture, they were unaccustomed to operating in this new environment. Welch wanted his managers to take charge of their businesses, make decisions, and take risks, but many of them were used to the protection offered by a heavily bureaucratic environment where decision making could be kicked upstairs. Many managers simply lacked the training or skills necessary to be effective. Others, who had climbed to the upper levels of the hierarchy, felt that their positions of authority were threatened and saw the power they had amassed over the years disappearing as the ground shifted underneath them.

Welch discovered that managers who seemed to buy in to his new vision for the company often went back to their desks and continued doing things in the same old way. Eventually some of them would be replaced. Many others were sent to GE's Crotonville management training center, where they began to acquire the skills and absorb the values necessary to succeed in the new corporate culture. The training program included, among other things, a series of experiential activities that operated on an emotional level to teach managers how to take risks, work together in teams, and acquire the perspectives and attitudes that would make them effective change agents. Through the Work Out program, salaried and hourly employees in a specific GE business came to Crotonville to jointly discuss problems and propose concrete solutions. At the end of the training session, they would present the proposals to their bosses, who were required to make an immediate decision on them. Reports had persisted at GE that many of these top managers were still resisting the change effort, although they were giving lip service to it. The Work Out program put them on the spot in front of their peers and subordinates—they couldn't hide any longer. It also underscored Welch's strong belief in empowerment at all levels of the organization to achieve the company's goals.

Welch came regularly to Crotonville, where he talked about the ideology that formed the keystone of the new corporate culture and fielded the questions put to him by GE managers. This ideology included the principle that each business must be number one or number two in its field. In addition, it totally redefined the relationship between the company and its employees. There was no longer any job security except what was provided by satisfied customers. Another element of Welch's ideology was that change was endless, "accepted as the rule rather than the exception."

The revolution that Welch inaugurated is continuing. What he appears to have accomplished—transforming a culture—is unquestionably the most difficult task confronting any CEO, even someone as obviously talented and energetic as Welch. Downsizing and restructuring, reengineering and team building are much easier and require far less perseverance, which is the reason so many corporate change processes go no further. Unfortunately, it's not enough.

Culture must be transformed as well. But this means dealing with issues of power and human nature, which are always complex and often extremely resistant to change.

# 3

# The Limits of Ideals and Vision Statements

In 1799, textile manufacturer Robert Owen and his partners purchased New Lanark, a mill town of sixteen hundred families located on the banks of the river Clyde in Scotland. New Lanark epitomized the worst conditions of the Industrial Revolution, which were to be so vividly portrayed several decades later in the novels of Charles Dickens. The workers in the giant cotton mill were mostly women and small children, many of them paupers rented from nearby poorhouses, whose nimble fingers toiled for twelve hours a day in dimly lit, dusty conditions.

Outside the factory walls, New Lanark's families lived in grinding poverty, victimized by their employers, who paid them low wages and then turned around and sold them life's necessities at exorbitant prices at the company store. Sanitary conditions in the town were primitive, and many people were laid waste by the ravages of disease. Others were forced to give up their jobs after being horribly mangled by the huge spinning machines, and still others, looking for a temporary escape, succumbed to alcoholism or drug addiction.

In less than two decades, Owen transformed this nightmare into the most famous model industrial town in England. He reduced working hours, improved housing, provided free medical services to keep his employees healthy, and offered free lectures in the evenings to improve their minds. Owen firmly believed that human beings were entirely products of their environment and their early training, and so he opened Britain's first kindergartens, calling them Institutions for the Formation of Character. At the same time, he also outlawed taverns in New Lanark and instituted fines for drunkenness—a further effort to control the environment and thereby reshape human behavior.

While Owen achieved impressive results with his experiment at New Lanark, he was not content to end it there. He hoped to expand the concept by establishing a series of model communities based on socialist principles that would emancipate workers from what Owen regarded as their enslavement to the machine. Unlike New Lanark, these communities would be totally self-sufficient in agriculture and manufactures, eliminating landlords and middlemen, who only preyed upon unfortunate wage earners, forcing them to work such long hours.

Owen confidently looked forward to the day when people would be "ready to commence a new empire upon the principle of public property and to discard private property."

In the winter of 1825, Owen purchased New Harmony, located on the banks of the Wabash River in Indiana, which he boldly predicted would be his first model commune. He gave speeches colorfully outlining his vision of a community where all people would be equal, share equally in the fruits of their toil, and work according to their own inclinations to do so. Advertisements appeared in the local newspapers urging people to pack up their belongings and move to New Harmony. And many responded. But as Owen's son reported, they were not the true believers that his father expected—they were more like a "heterogeneous collection of radicals, enthusiastic devotees to principles, honest latitudinarians, and lazy theorists with a sprinkling of unprincipled sharpers thrown in."

Since all the inhabitants were free to do whatever they wanted, some worked, but others puttered around aimlessly, doing nothing. Owen, who had invested most of his life's savings in the enterprise, neglected to give it the leadership and organization needed to carry out the activities that would eventually make New Harmony self-sufficient. Unlike New Lanark, which was tightly controlled by Owen and his managers, each decision in this new community had to be put to a vote. Indeed, one observer explained that the inhabitants spent more time voting than they did farming or running the community's small manufacturing activities, so very little work was ever accomplished.

Anyone who disagreed with the outcome of the voting could simply leave the community, and many did. Some inhabitants left when Owen prohibited drinking. Others decided that they didn't support the notion of equality, for it forced them to hobnob with those they believed were socially beneath them. Still others packed up when Owen tried to ban money and replace it with labor notes. While he proudly proclaimed to the outside world that the "principle of union and cooperation . . . is now universally admitted to be far superior to the individual selfish system," New Harmony collapsed in a wail of discord.

## *Ideals and the Realities of Human Nature*

Owen's experiments at New Lanark and New Harmony seem to illustrate the limits of ideals. In Scotland, he successfully carried out an altruistic program to uplift the lives of his workers, but within the narrow context of a traditional capitalist enterprise firmly focused on the bottom line. In Indiana, by contrast, he was attempting nothing less than the creation of a totally new economic and social order. While this may have been a noble ideal, he failed to provide it with sufficient leadership. Even more important, it was based upon totally unrealistic expectations of human nature and, therefore, doomed to failure.

Like Robert Owen's vision for New Harmony, today's corporate vision statements are often filled with lofty ideals designed to inspire employees to remake the organization. Ideals can offer a direction to follow that promotes real progress, but they can also undo an entire change effort. Why?

Sometimes they are based on a view of human nature that is far too idealized to be realistic. Even if some of the ideals are realizable, carrying them out may be a herculean task that will take many years to accomplish and require constant dedication by all levels of an organization. Unfortunately, no one ever makes this entirely clear to the employees. Nor is management really prepared to make the long-term commitment necessary to make these idealistic values an integral part of the corporate culture. Instead, the ideals are simply promulgated—often with the best of intentions, but when a company's reach falls far short of its grasp, top managers visibly lose interest in their lofty value statements, employees become discouraged and cynical, and, as a result, the change effort quickly loses its momentum.

Several years ago, the corporate vice president charged with running a large subsidiary of a major manufacturing company was asked to prepare a report showing how well he had carried out the company's new quality improvement process. The program, which was barely two years old, had been based on a series of values that included satisfying the expectations of the customer, respect for the individual, community outreach, and employee empowerment. The vice president promptly summoned his immediate subordinates and directed them to write detailed summaries of the progress they had achieved in promoting the quality program in their departments. A few weeks later, after they had submitted their written statements, he gathered them together in a sprawling conference room. Following some introductory remarks, he went around the table and, one by one, systematically ripped each of his managers to shreds because each of their summaries had failed to satisfy him. He eventually threw all of them in the wastepaper basket and wrote the entire report himself. So much for employee empowerment!

In retrospect, perhaps it had been unreasonable to expect this vice president to act any differently. After all, he was a grizzled veteran of the old school who had been used to an autocratic approach to management. The veneer of the new quality improvement process, with its emphasis on empowerment, was still very thin, and its principles hadn't really penetrated his leathery hide. Nor was there any compelling reason for him to adopt these principles. In the past, his superiors had apparently been pleased with his success regardless of his management style, and they didn't seem to be applying much pressure on him to operate any differently. So it was natural for him to hold firmly on to his executive power and resist change. Unhappily, it was just as natural for his subordinates to believe that all the talk about empowerment was just that: talk. And they probably began to lose faith in the quality process.

## Ideologies That Overlook Human Nature

"Been there. Done that. Got the mug. Got the T-shirt. Ho hum." It's the reaction heard everywhere from weary employees, upon being told that top management is planning still another change effort. And yet, every year, consultants appear on the scene with a new ideology designed to revolutionize an organization.

One of the most popular recently has been described by its champions as a form of corporate democracy, expressed through self-directed work teams requiring only minimal direction from a central command structure. Employees have the freedom to form teams as necessary to work on specific projects or deal with special problems as they arise. Whether these problems are strictly internal or relate to the needs of the customer, teams of people close to the situation will be able to act rapidly and intelligently to deal with it—at least, so say the experts who are proposing this type of corporate environment. In this culture, teams from different functional areas will readily cooperate with one another as they work together on a project. And once the project has been completed, the teams will voluntarily disband, and their members will be free to join other teams to deal with new problems.

While these management gurus are very long on their description of an idealized work environment, they are very short on the process necessary to get there. And yet corporations are often urged to chart their destinies by these types of ideals. Can we assume, for instance, that employees from different functional areas will naturally communicate clearly and openly without any misperceptions of one another's motives, fear of hidden agendas, petty jealousies between their leaders, or turf battles? Can we be sure that they will put aside their own parochial viewpoints and recognize the best interests of the entire organization? And once each project has been completed, will they disband their teams, voluntarily relinquishing the prestige or power they may have achieved in the organization? All of this seems to imply a level of perfectiblility that lies beyond the grasp of most human beings, at least without a great deal of retraining.

Suppose a chemical company wants teams from sales and manufacturing to prepare a joint action plan aimed at improving customer relations. Each team brings to the table its own perceptions filtered through its own individual set of experiences. Sales hears customer complaints that chemicals are not always up to specifications and shipments are sometimes late. The salespeople blame manufacturing for these problems and believe that it is incapable of doing the job properly. The manufacturing team, on the other hand, has a totally different perception: It blames the salespeople for promising far more than the company can deliver in order to close a sale. However, the manufacturing people are afraid they won't receive a fair hearing on this issue; they think that because the new CEO is the former vice president for sales, he will naturally take the side of the sales department. The manufacturing team is, therefore, feeling very defensive, certain that the salespeople look down their noses at them as a group of insensitive engineers.

On the other side of the table, the members of the sales team also find themselves in a tight spot. They have not been meeting their quotas lately, and they believe that the new CEO may begin to fire some of them if this situation is not improved—after all, he can't be perceived as being unduly partial to the members of his former functional area. In addition, the salespeople think that the technical people in manufacturing feel superior to them because they aren't as highly educated. They also believe that some of the engineers do not want to share all the relevant information about their chemical processes because they're unwilling to lose control of their own turf.

These are just some of the issues that may pose obstacles to a smooth exchange of ideas between sales and manufacturing. They represent the fundamental elements of human nature that must be dealt with if cross-functional teams are to work successfully. Of course, we know from our own experience that in some organizations under some circumstances, teams can open up the clogged arteries of decrepit bureaucracies and achieve spectacular results. Clearly, employees can work together across functional areas; what's more, they can do it very effectively.

But does this mean that the same concept can work everywhere? Is it the panacea that can revitalize any area of any organization?

## A Problem With Ideals

A major problem with ideals is that they usually seem to be stated in terms of absolutes: Flatter is always better! Teams are the best vehicle for producing change! Employee empowerment is essential to our success! Nothing is that simple. If it were, corporations would be far easier to run. The fact is that organizations often operate in a state of dynamic tension between opposing points of view. A manager may generally believe in empowering a work team to make its own decisions. But suppose that team seems headed in the wrong direction. Should the manager let the situation play itself out and preserve the ideal of empowerment? Or should he or she intervene? Time and time again, managers have lamented that they didn't intervene soon enough.

Management is not an exact science, like mathematics; it is closer to psychotherapy, where there are generally no right or wrong answers, just theories—and hundreds of them, at that. Perhaps to an even greater extent than psychotherapy, the study of organizations is only in its infancy. We simply don't have the database to say with any confidence what works or what doesn't, and (even more importantly) why. Did Company A improve its performance because employees were empowered and networks of self-managed teams began to honeycomb the organization? Or did the improvement result from a general upturn in the economy, or in the market niche in which the company does business? Or was the improvement due to the dynamic leadership of the CEO? Or the invention of a new product? Or some combination of all these factors? Or another variable that we haven't even uncovered?

In order to answer these questions, we'd have to select a large sample of companies, implement the same change process in each of them, examine the results, and compare them to a control sample where we did nothing. Needless to say, that type of information does not exist.

## Ideals and the Realities of Power

Many of the corporate values statements that are supposed to guide large-scale change efforts appear to have been developed without acknowledging the realities of power. The fact is that some individuals are intensely driven by motives such as power and individual achievement, seemingly to the exclusion of almost anything else. To confirm this view of human nature, we need only look at history, which is filled with remarkable figures such as Napoleon and Franklin Roosevelt, Catherine the Great and Winston Churchill—people who were obsessed with acquiring individual power and compiling a record of extraordinary accomplishment. In his book, *The Inner World of Abraham Lincoln,* Michael Burlingame describes a man who—contrary to the popular myth—was extremely ambitious. After repeatedly failing to win a Senate seat, Lincoln persisted in his pursuit of power until he was finally elected president in 1860.

People with personalities of this type abound inside organizations and frequently rise to the top to become senior vice presidents and even CEOs. Indeed, reward and recognition systems have usually been designed to encourage individual achievement and promote managers who wanted to acquire additional power. These reward systems may have changed in recent years to recognize team accomplishment and encourage employees to become team players. But it would be naive to assume that human nature has suddenly changed. As they have since the beginning of the species, some humans still crave power and, once they have achieved it, want to hold onto it.

Several years ago, Peter Brill was asked by the director of a large museum to help her deal with a crisis in her organization. A depressed economy in the region had led to a decline in the number of patrons and weakening financial support for her institution. She realized that her management team was becoming demoralized, and that several departments were already engaged in open warfare, blaming one another for the museum's worsening problems. In an effort to defuse this situation, Brill led the managers through a three-day program; by the end of it, all of them had agreed on approximately twenty key measures that they would undertake together to improve the museum's position.

At this point, Brill stood up on stage with the director. "Now, all of us are in complete agreement about where we want to go," he said, "and what we're going to do in the coming weeks." All the managers were nodding their heads. It had been a long and tiring session, but ultimately a successful one.

Then, he turned to the director. "Oh, no, we're not," she said.

Apparently, several recommendations did not meet with her approval, and she intended to use all of her power to block them.

## First Principle of Power: People Who Have Power Usually Do Not Give it Up Voluntarily

Anyone who doubts the truth of this statement simply has to ask Congressional Republicans who endured forty years of Democratic control in the United States House of Representatives before the 1994 elections, or talk to the thousands of women who, unlike our museum director, have been unsuccessful in their efforts to break through the glass ceiling that exists inside many organizations. Power means control. It bestows prestige and privilege, perks that are far too seductive for most people to relinquish willingly.

Managers may give lip service to the principles of empowerment, but the reality is often quite different, making the transition process difficult. Many a department head who tries to change procedures in his or her organization has learned this lesson the hard way. Outwardly all of the managers may agree with the reforms, but in reality they often see them as a threat to their way of doing things. As a result, the reforms may never be implemented.

Another factor also helps to explain the reluctance of many managers to change: They often feel uncomfortable in a new culture because they lack the necessary tools to function there effectively. It's similar to doing business in a country that you've never seen before. The new culture is totally unfamiliar, and you have no model for what is expected of you. Eventually, you may acquire a model, but even then you still must figure out how to translate it into specific behaviors on your job. Once you know what these behaviors are, you have to practice them so that they feel natural. And when you do begin to practice them, you have to rely on your colleagues to do the same thing or the entire operation may be jeopardized. If you successfully get over this hurdle, you still must depend on the rest of the organization to support your efforts. And, finally, you may need to learn how to interface with other departments where the change process has not yet started.

This is a tough situation and may explain why so many managers are reluctant to embrace the brave new world of corporate change.

## Second Principle of Power:
## Hierarchies Are the Natural Order of Things

As organizations try to flatten out their hierarchies, they need to ask themselves an important question: What purpose is the hierarchy designed to serve? In their book *Reframing Organizations,* Bolman and Deal contrast the organizational structures at McDonald's and at Harvard University. The former is tightly controlled from the top, with a long chain of command that reaches into every restaurant and down to every employee in order to ensure uniformity—a hamburger at one location is to be the same as a hamburger everywhere else. By contrast, Harvard is a far more decentralized organization, with each school largely in control of its own destiny and every professor teaching according to his or her own unique style. People want individuality from the Harvard faculty, but not from McDonald's hamburger flippers.

For each organization, there seems to be an optimal degree of command structure. This varies with the purpose of the organization and the amount of alignment required among the employees. One CEO explained that he had reduced his hierarchy from six management levels to three, which was very low for his industry, but that this was about as far as he could take it. Someone had to make the decisions, he said, and the staff needed someone they could relate to as the boss. Cutting layers of management just for the sake of cutting may undermine the functioning of your organization. Instead, it is essential to find the proper amount of hierarchy to promote efficiency.

Incidentally, hierarchies will always exist because they seem to be a natural organizing principle of life. Mammals form dominance hierarchies, for example. The human family is a hierarchy consisting of parents and children. The human body is also organized hierarchically, with single cells making up more complex tissues that combine to form even more complex organs, such as the heart and the brain.

In fact, organizations that eliminate layers of formal hierarchy usually discover that informal structures emerge to replace them. These may form around natural leaders, like the people that Terrence Deal and Allen Kennedy describe in their classic study, *Corporate Cultures*. These leaders may be the mavericks who direct successful skunk works or the corporate heroes who lead the organization into new markets. They attract their own followers, who establish hierarchies of their own that exist side by side with the formal organization chart.

## Third Principle of Power:
## In Each Organization There Are Different Types of Power

Inside every organization, power is clothed in various forms and resides in different centers. Successful change often depends on persuading enough powerful people to buy into a transition process. *Formal* power, of course, is described in your company's organization chart, which tells you the people in authority who are charged with enforcing the rules. While their support is critical, it is only the beginning, because there are many types of informal power that may prove just as important.

These include *moral* power, which carries the force of sanctions against any employee who violates the values of the culture. Moral power may be exercised by the individuals that Deal and Kennedy call priests: those who preserve the institution and its hallowed traditions. Since any change effort generally strikes at these traditions, the priests and their followers may be expected to oppose it unless you can enlist their enthusiastic approval.

*Expertise* is another kind of power, usually represented by various gurus and wannabes, who can be found in almost any functional area. These are employees who possess outstanding reputations that have won them wide respect throughout the organization, and so their support can be crucial.

Finally, there is *coercive* power. This is the ultimate authority to hire and fire, to determine corporate strategy and change organizational structures. This form of power resides in people like the CEO and other top managers. The leader may need to use coercive power to initiate the change process, especially if he or she is the only one who seems to recognize the necessity for change. There may simply be no other way for the leader to start the ball rolling than by announcing his or her vision for the organization to the members of the management team. Then the leader must be skilled at reaching out to all of the opinion makers in the organization—those who possess expert power and moral power as well as those who hold positions of authority in the company's formal organization chart. This process requires the leader to have the ability to persuade others that he or she is fully committed to the change process, the ability to set an example and undertake actions that seem consistent with the process, and a past record of success, which enhances his or her reputation throughout the organization. This is the leader's own moral and expert power. The leader cannot rely on coercive power alone to force change down employees' throats, because resistance will build that can undermine the entire process. Smart leaders understand this, and use this power only sparingly, when there seems to be no alternative.

The CEO of a major manufacturing company was trying to direct his organization through a painful change process. He had given speeches championing employee empowerment, reduced layers of management and flattened the hierarchy, guided the reorganization of various departments into self-managed work teams, and led his immediate subordinates through strategic planning programs to capitalize on new market opportunities. But while all of his top managers gave lip service to the new culture, some of them still remained unconvinced. Finally, the CEO exploded a bombshell: He fired two of his vice presidents because they had repeatedly tried to undermine what he was trying to accomplish. The CEO realized that he probably should have taken this step much sooner, but he was afraid of creating shock waves throughout the entire corporation. These two managers commanded the loyalty of a large number of devoted employees, and the CEO was afraid that by firing both of them, he would create enormous resistance to his change effort. Unfortunately, he had simply run out of other options.

## The Role of Vision Statements

One of the primary purposes of a vision statement or a list of values that make up a corporate ideology is to enable the leader to cloak the use of power in terms of a business imperative and thus maintain the moral high ground. Instead of simply ordering that something be done, the leader can say that it must be done for the sake of carrying out the mission of the organization. Jack Welch, for example, redefined the mission of GE. He insisted that an impending crisis could be averted only if each business made itself number one or number two in its market. This gave him the moral authority he needed to engineer a cataclysmic upheaval at GE, which involved laying off thousands and thousands of employees.

As Eccles and Nohria point out in their book *Beyond the Hype*, skillful leaders know how to use words effectively "to give meaning to their actions . . . to build momentum for the actions they desire and opposition for the actions they wish to block." Welch has relied on rhetoric time and again to help him transform GE.

He began with the rule of number one and number two, using it to destabilize the system, as we discussed in the previous chapter. This ideology was also powerful enough to captivate and motivate employees, without being used to discredit Welch's leadership. It tapped deeply into the competitive juices of many GE managers, while clearly positioning the company very well strategically. How could a GEer really attack Welch for setting such a goal? The most anyone could say was that Welch was being unrealistic, that what he was asking for simply couldn't be done. But once some of the businesses actually met his standards, even this argument evaporated. In fact, the failure of the others to reach the same goal simply revealed the weakness of their managers or their business, not the unfairness of the CEO in establishing such benchmarks. Therefore, every manager would now feel compelled to measure up to Welch's standards, and his ideology became self-reinforcing—one of the critical factors in making the change process.

Finally, an ideology must be powerful emotionally and strategically without being too specific right from the outset. Welch, for example, started with the rule of number one and number two. Only later did he add to the corporate ideology terms like *workout, integrated diversity,* and the *boundaryless organization.* All of these ideals, while inspirational, were also general enough so that GEers could interpret them in a variety of ways and apply them to many different practical situations.

The problem with many corporate vision statements is that they're too specific, too idealistic, right from the beginning of the change process. This is often a recipe for failure. As change begins, it is usually impossible to determine which values will be most important in carrying out corporate strategy. If a set of values is announced with a great deal of corporate fanfare, only to fall by the wayside later, the rank-and-file employees will become disenchanted. And who can blame them?

A more successful approach may be to begin with a single principle, one that may not even sound like a vision statement at all: "Each business should be number one or number two in its market." "Do what is right for the customer." Such a broad, general statement can encompass a wide range of activities. As the change process proceeds, experience will begin to tell leaders which activities and which values are important in carrying out the corporate vision. Each of these values can be promulgated later and closely tied to the overarching vision. Once this happens, however, a leader must be prepared to use all the forms of power at her or his disposal to ensure that they are incorporated into every level of the organization. Otherwise, the values and the vision statement will lose their meaning for employees.

## A Vision Statement That Works

From its very earliest days, a successful managed health care company had been guided by a single, broad principle: Do what is right for the customer. Since the company runs employee assistance programs and handles case management for large corporations, the customers were the corporations themselves as well as their workers. Over the years, two additional values were added to the first principle: The team concept and lifelong learning for every employee.

Today, these values have permeated throughout the entire culture, in large part due to the vigorous efforts of the firm's CEO. But he didn't arrive at all of them easily. Like almost everything else, they had to be learned the hard way. For example, during the early years of the organization, the CEO had championed a star culture: Nurture a few talented individuals, he believed, and they would provide effective leadership for their subordinates. What he discovered was that these stars also built their own fiefdoms, demanding that each member of their staff put loyalty to them ahead of their commitment to the organization. This lead to disruptive power struggles within the firm and a serious threat of fragmentation. Finally the CEO was forced to fire one of his talented vice presidents when she threatened to undermine an important change effort he had initiated that would have enabled the firm to enter a new market.

This experience acted as a catalyst, helping to convince the CEO that the firm must be transformed into a team-based culture. But it proved to be a long process. The CEO constantly reiterated the importance of this value in meetings and conversations with employees; teams were collectively recognized and rewarded for their contributions to successful projects, instead of individual employees being singled out with special bonuses; cross-functional teams were encouraged throughout the organization.

Perhaps most importantly, the CEO made it clear that he would not tolerate any effort by one department to blame another for a problem. What does this mean in practice? Suppose a case manager is heard to say, "Oh, those marketing people. It's their fault we're getting complaints from this customer. They promised more than we can deliver." That case manager would be required to attend a meeting of the marketing staff and repeat her complaint in front of them. This is usually enough to convince a staff member that the "blame game" is simply unacceptable. Instead, employees must consider every problem as a problem that involves everyone, calling for teamwork and cooperation, putting the needs of the firm and its commitment to the customer ahead of everything else.

These values are clearly communicated to employees right from the beginning. The CEO, for example, participates in hiring interviews, where he describes the firm's culture to prospective employees and urges them to think carefully about whether they can fully subscribe to its guiding principles. These are his values, he explains, and they are so deeply ingrained in the firm's culture that anyone who doesn't support them will be ostracized by coworkers.

He or she may also be without a job. On one occasion, a case manager received a telephone call in the middle of the night from a patient with a dire emergency. The manager refused to listen to the problem and hung up the phone. This incident was eventually brought to the attention of the CEO, who immediately asked for an explanation. When the case manager tried to rationalize his behavior and downplay its significance, the CEO pointed out that the manager had violated the values of the company—his values—and promptly fired him.

A third principle of this organization is lifelong learning. Since the health care field is changing rapidly, employees must constantly update their skills to remain current with the marketplace. While members of the firm seem to recognize the need for personal growth at least on an intellectual level, the everyday pressures of work may prevent them from devoting enough time to developing new skills. They may also be afraid to confront the risk of failure that the learning process often involves. The CEO realizes that one of his most important tasks is pushing people to learn and take risks so that they can grow. "We won't come down on you if you fail," he tells everyone, "only if you don't try."

At this firm, corporate values are more than just talk; they are tightly woven into the fabric of the organization, where they form a living, breathing framework for doing business. But this culture has taken years to develop, beginning with a single, broad principle and later adding others, often through trial and error. The firm's success is due, in large part, to the gradual evolution of its practical ideals and the strong support they receive from employees. A final key element is the leadership of a CEO who is dedicated to living and working by these corporate values and utilizing his power to ensure that they are followed consistently throughout the organization.

# Part Two
# The Four Levers

# 4

# The Human Factor

If you had lived in one of the quiet villages of Nottinghamshire in the English Midlands during the fall of 1811, your life would have been disrupted by bizarre activities. Roving bands of marauders wielding rifles and large hammers were breaking into the shops of local hosiery manufacturers at night and destroying the new wide frames on which stockings were mass-produced. These outlaws were followers of a mythical "General Ludd," who reputedly lived in Sherwood Forest. The Luddites, as they called themselves, belonged to a secret society—with secret passwords, signs, and even a song to accompany their nightly work of destruction.

*And by night when all is still*
*And the moon is hid behind the hill*
*We forward march to do our will*
*With hatchet, pike and gun!*

Who were the Luddites? Workers in the stocking trade—journeymen and apprentices operating hand looms for their bosses, who were master stockingers, and who had rented the looms from the hosiers. These stocking workers were craftsmen, used to producing high-quality, finely styled stockings. Unfortunately, they were also members of a dying trade. The stocking market was changing; hosiers were now demanding mass-produced, lower-quality stockings and were willing to pay far less for them. Wages declined, and the workers saw their hours cut. Then the hosiers introduced the wide frames, which would enable them to produce even more stockings faster and with even fewer operators. Seeing their livelihoods in jeopardy and being forced to reduce the quality of their products, the workers eventually began to demonstrate. When this didn't work, they turned to violence.

Gradually, the insurrection spread northward to Yorkshire and Lancashire, where industrialization had also forced craftsmen into unemployment. Here the Luddites attacked the factories that housed the huge cotton power looms and wool shearing machines. They pummeled these devices with their hammers, killing armed guards whom the owners had hired to protect their factories and, in some instances, burning the factories themselves.

When troops of regulars were sent north to stop the Luddites, the local townspeople at first tried to protect these erstwhile Robin Hoods, many of whom were their own kin. But there was little support for them in Parliament, which regarded industrialization as a boon to the British economy and even passed a law making destruction of the looms punishable by execution. Eventually, the ringleaders were rounded up, tried, and hanged or transported to penal colonies overseas. The revolt ended. But the example of the Luddites has not been forgotten, and they are still regarded as ignorant workers with an irrational, shortsighted attitude toward change.

Shortsighted? Certainly. Irrational? Unquestionably. But isn't this a natural human reaction to the change process?

Luddites exist in every organization. Perhaps it's an employee on the factory floor who intentionally tries to undermine a reengineering project by his work team because he's afraid it may cost him his job. Or maybe it's the purchasing manager who's reluctant to institute tighter performance measurements because they will expose the inadequacies of her operation. If change is the natural order of things in modern organizations, so, apparently, is resistance. Indeed, a study conducted by the Center for Creative Leadership found that only 25 percent of employees embrace the change process. The rest try to actively stonewall it or "talk the talk" without really "walking the walk."

Unfortunately, this problem cannot be overcome simply through a reasoned discussion in which a manager logically presents the merits of a change initiative. One CEO ruefully explained that he had learned from bitter experience that logical arguments were not enough to convince skeptical employees they ought to change their way of doing things. "Logic is important," the CEO said, "but the most important thing is getting it into their hearts."

Change must occur at the emotional level—the same place where resistance to change usually occurs. It's a battle for the hearts of employees, and if you lose that battle, the transformation process will encounter barriers that may prove insurmountable. Too many CEOs and other top managers have learned this lesson the hard way.

## *Trouble in Paradise*

At a sprawling golf and tennis resort nestled among rolling hills that slope gently toward the warm Caribbean waters, a young general manager was working sixteen-hour days to achieve his vision: world-class status. For decades, the resort management had been content to drift lazily from season to season, like the huge palm trees that covered the magnificent landscape. A group of immensely wealthy homeowners whose plush villas surrounded the resort supported the cost of maintaining the golf course, the large hotel that catered to tourists, and the beaches. The villa owners had seemed unconcerned by the fact that these costs kept rising year after year. This was their playground, a quiet retreat where they could display their wealth and cavort with their friends; money meant nothing to them.

Indeed, the attitude of the homeowners appeared to shape the culture of the entire resort. While the staff were efficient and interested in serving the needs of the guests, they were decidedly independent and suspicious of any attempt to control them, for they regarded this luxury property as their own fiefdom. When the homeowners would suggest some changes in the operations, senior staff members would simply smile and nod their heads, only to report a few weeks later that these things were impossible.

The operation of the resort had remained almost unchanged for many years, until some of the older homeowners died or sold their villas. They were gradually replaced by a younger generation of self-made multimillionaires. These were people who had grown rich running efficient businesses, with a keen eye to the bottom line. They resented the fact that their assessments to maintain the property kept rising year after year, and they finally refused to hand over an additional dollar to the resort's management until they could examine the books. What they discovered there appalled them: a mismanaged operation where food and beverage costs, groundskeeping costs, and hotel maintenance expenses were spiraling out of control. They immediately brought in new management.

The young manager, who had trained at some of the world's best hotels, saw this as a unique opportunity to introduce new procedures that had proved successful elsewhere. He hired a consulting firm to help him pinpoint the areas of greatest deficiency and recommend possible solutions. Then he sat down with the senior members of the resort staff and discussed the changes that needed to occur. They seemed to agree with what he proposed, the manager explained. Then, he told us, they went off and intentionally misinterpreted what he had said to their subordinates.

"Why?" we asked him.

"Change meant that they were going to lose control," he explained, "and they wanted to protect themselves."

Together, the senior staffers and their subordinates "demonized" him, the new manager recalled. They turned him into the enemy, undermined his authority, and, as an act of blatant defiance, even punctured the tires on his car. He tried training programs, designed to persuade the employees that change was essential and to teach them the skills they needed to function in a new environment. But the training was ineffective because the senior staffers continued to feel threatened. Finally, the manager was forced to fire them and bring in a new group of supervisors.

The change process at this resort is still continuing. The manager has hired more consultants, who are recommending a new round of training for the staff. And he is confident of eventual success. Perhaps he will succeed. If the employees learn a new set of skills, their mindset and attitudes may change, too.

But anecdotal evidence from several staff members suggests that this may not be enough. An atmosphere of fear now pervades the organization. Many employees still resent the manager, and several of them said they don't respect his judgment or the ability of his new management team to run the resort. Can these employees be won over? Or has the manager lost the battle for their hearts? Will his use of raw power simply create new centers of resistance, forcing him to fire even more people and endure a high rate of turnover for the foreseeable future? And how will this affect the operation of the resort?

Finally, will he continue to receive the support of the homeowners, or will they grow impatient and call for a new manager?

## Human Nature and Resistance to Change

This story portrays some of the negative reactions that might be expected from human beings who are confronted with change. Since the change process is extremely disruptive, it should come as no surprise that not everyone rushes to embrace it with open arms.

Try to recall your own feelings the last time you were forced to move and start over again, leaving behind a comfortable home where everything was familiar and arranged just the way you wanted it, a neighborhood where you had made close friends, a school that your children enjoyed attending, and a community where your family experienced a sense of belonging.

At one level, organizational change is very similar because it involves a loss of the familiar, with all of the attendant feelings that accompany it.

Just as someone who moves to a new community must adjust to unfamiliar surroundings, employees involved in a change process must deal with new structures and learn new procedures. Something as simple as opening a new customer account, for example, or receiving a shipping order may have to be done entirely differently, producing uncomfortable feelings of awkwardness and anxiety for employees as they learn the ropes.

Change often involves the introduction of complex and unfamiliar technology that alters not only the way a company does business, but the very nature of the business itself, frequently requiring employees to redefine who they are and what they do in their offices each day. At a large textbook company that was making the transition from print to electronic publishing, editors who had spent their entire careers writing and designing for the printed page were being forced to adjust to the brave new world of CD-ROM. Long considered masters of their field, these experienced editors now felt awkward trying to learn the new computer skills they needed for electronic publishing. They didn't like losing their accustomed feeling of mastery and suddenly finding themselves at the bottom of a learning curve. It undermined their position of influence, which had been usurped by a group of young programmers who were leading the charge into CD-ROM.

Change often involves power shifts in an organization, with some people losing visibility and others, whose skills enable them to thrive in the new business environment, rising to prominence. When people feel their power and control slipping away, it's natural for them to react by throwing up defenses or attacking the source of the problem, like the employees at the golf resort who demonized the new general manager and punctured his tires.

A similar response occurred when a new secretary of human services in a large eastern state was charged by the governor who appointed him with streamlining the operations of his department. The bureaucrats, who had served there for years, had seen other hotshot secretaries try the same thing, and they knew just how to deal with it. Each of them had developed an area of expertise governed by an elaborate set of procedures that no one else understood. When the new secretary directed them to make some change, they didn't directly oppose him; they simply did nothing. If he tried to maneuver around them, he couldn't, because he didn't understand how to accomplish anything in their areas. Thus they protected their power and stonewalled his efforts.

In his book *Groups in Conflict*, Kerwyn K. Smith describes what happens when an atmosphere of defensiveness becomes pervasive, as it did in the state Department of Human Services and the luxury golf resort. Smith examines the roles of three groups that exist in every organization: the Elites, the Ins, and the Outs.

The Elites are the people at the top of the hierarchy, those with the ultimate power to hire and fire, like the homeowners at the resort or the governor who appointed the secretary of human services. The Ins are expected to carry out the directives of the Elites—the new general manager was supposed to improve the efficiency of the resort; the new secretary was charged with overhauling his department. The Outs are the remainder of the employees, those who see themselves left out of the hierarchy of power and who are expected to do the bidding of the Elites and the Ins.

As Smith points out, each group has a particular view of the world that is largely determined by its position in the hierarchy. Since the Elites believe that they hold all the power, they expect their wishes to be obeyed by the Ins and the Outs. Furthermore, they are usually intolerant of any excuses from the Ins for their inability to carry out the Elites' directives. Unfortunately, the Ins frequently find themselves caught between the Elites and the Outs, unable to satisfy either group. For example, while the Ins may direct the Outs to do something, there is no guarantee that they will actually do it. For the Outs have their own view of the organization—often a suspicious and defensive view, a belief that everything the Elites and the Ins do is simply an attempt to exercise power over them. Like the bureaucrats in the Department of Human Services or the staff people at the resort, they frequently try to resist any change effort, and the entire system may be locked in stalemate. Unless the system can be unlocked, the transformation process may fail.

Thus resistance inside an organization is a very natural human response that may have a variety of causes. These might include pure self-interest, a lack of trust in the people in power, a low tolerance for change, or very little confidence that the effort will actually work. Regardless of its origin, the impact may be the same: failure to achieve long-lasting improvements.

## Human Nature and Support for Change

Having described some of the negative responses to change, we don't wish to overlook the fact that human beings are also capable of expending enormous energy in support of corporate renewal. Many employees have willingly taken salary cuts, worked longer hours, sacrificed their personal lives, and even spent their life's savings to purchase their company, all in the hope of rescuing a failing enterprise and effecting a turnaround. Call this eternal optimism, if you want, or even cockeyed idealism, but it has the power to move mountains, to say nothing of saving an organization from the corporate scrap heap.

This is the spirit that sustains soldiers on the battlefield, stirring them to glorious charges in the face of a seemingly invincible enemy. Think of the second day at the battle of Gettysburg, when Joshua Chamberlain's regiment, the Twentieth Maine Volunteers, had run out of ammunition, yet he led them on a courageous charge that preserved the Union Army's position at Little Round Top and prevented a Confederate victory that might have changed the outcome of the Civil War. This was the same spirit that inspired the 1951 New York Giants when they came from 13½ games back to defeat the Brooklyn Dodgers for the National League pennant on Bobby Thomson's incredible home run.

Why do these events move us so deeply? Simply because they strike a resonant chord in the human psyche. Our employees are no different. They're also capable of performing successful feats in the face of enormous odds, and making last-minute efforts that save the day. They want something to cheer about and believe in.

In the late 1970s, as the Big Three automakers were being counted out, most of top management was busy wringing its hands or trying to boost sagging sales with more of the same tired remedies that had already proved unsuccessful. But a small group of intrepid executives dared to defy the prevailing logic and advocate a new way of doing things, preaching the benefits of total quality, employee empowerment, and listening to the customers—the very approaches that had made the Japanese car companies so successful. Paul Ingrassia and Joseph B. White describe these unsung heroes in their book *Comeback: The Fall and Rise of the American Automobile Industry.* They were people who never lost faith and eventually helped lead another American revolution.

At a large paper mill in the Southeast, a management team had become demoralized by successive waves of layoffs and the tunnel vision of a new CEO who measured performance only in terms of the volume of product being shipped out the door, not the degree of customer satisfaction. The plant manager, a crusty veteran with many years of service to the company, had traveled repeatedly to corporate headquarters to meet with the CEO, yet he had been unsuccessful in persuading the CEO to readjust his priorities or recognize the damage he had inflicted on the pride of his employees. Instead of giving up, however, the plant manager decided to try a different approach.

He convened a meeting of his staff to watch a series of videotapes describing successful corporate turnarounds in organizations where the obstacles were no more formidable than those currently facing his plant. These tapes served as a catalyst, encouraging all those in the room to begin discussing what they could do to improve their operation. The staff began by looking at small projects where they could score some immediate successes. These would build enthusiasm among employees and restore morale. Each of the projects was spearheaded by an employee team. Early results were generally encouraging, and momentum for the process grew throughout the facility.

Meanwhile the plant manager and his immediate subordinates spent a weekend together in a wilderness experience. This strengthened the management team and increased their sense of mutual trust. Together, they began to shape more ambitious projects, convinced that they could continue to meet the CEO's demand for high volume while they rebuilt the spirit of their plant and turned it into a showcase for the entire corporation.

Will the manager and his team succeed? It's too early to tell. But it's a tribute to their optimism and their ability to overcome the bleak demoralization pervading the mill that they are even willing to try.

## *The Complexity of Human Beings*

It's easy to forget sometimes that employees are not one-dimensional creatures who park their human nature at the door when they enter the workplace. They are complex and paradoxical, a combination of soaring idealism and dark pessimism, stubborn short-sightedness and courageous vision, narrow-minded suspicion and open-handed trust, irrational revenge and tender unselfishness. In short, they are human beings.

Perhaps one of the clearest windows we have into the true nature of human beings is provided by those great novelists who fill their pages with unforgettable characters—unforgettable precisely because they are so human. In *The Great Gatsby*, for example, F. Scott Fitzgerald describes the first face-to-face meeting between the book's narrator, Nick Carraway, and his illustrious next-door neighbor, Jay Gatsby. The setting is Gatsby's huge estate on Long Island, where he is throwing a glittering party for his many acquaintances, and Carraway seems to realize almost instinctively that his host is a man of astounding contradictions.

> "I'm Gatsby," he said suddenly.
> "What!" I exclaimed. "Oh, I beg your pardon."
> "I thought you knew, old sport. I'm afraid I'm not a very good host."
> He smiled understandingly—much more than understandingly. It was one of those rare smiles with a quality of eternal reassurance in it, that you may come across four or five times in life. It faced—or seemed to face—the whole external world for an instant, and then concentrated on *you* with an irresistible prejudice in your favor. It understood you just as far as you wanted to be understood, believed in you as you would like to believe in yourself, and assured you that it had precisely the impression of you that, at your best, you hoped to convey. Precisely at that point it vanished—and I was looking at an elegant young roughneck, a year or two over thirty, whose elaborate formality of speech just missed being absurd.[1]

1. F. Scott Fitzgerald, *The Great Gatsby* (New York: Scribner's, 1925).

As we learn in the novel, Gatsby's contradictions don't stop here. The glittering showplace where he stages his magical parties is nothing more than a facade for a corrupt fortune earned from the brutal bootlegging business. Indeed, Gatsby is a creature who has taken advantage of the social change that shaped the Roaring Twenties. And yet the opulent lifestyle he has fashioned is primarily designed to make time stand still. Gatsby is using it to woo back his first love, Daisy Buchanan, who has since married and moved into a lavish mansion only a short distance away. Gatsby idealizes Daisy and hopes to recapture the past they had once enjoyed together. When Nick tries to tell him that this is impossible, the street-smart confidence man seems incredulous. "Can't repeat the past? Why, of course, you can!"

Although Gatsby ultimately fails, it is his quest for the ideal that sets him apart from all the other crass characters who populate Fitzgerald's novel. And Nick, who has initially disliked Gatsby, comes to admire him because he is such an idealist. As the critic David Parker explains, "Nick learns ... to accept the paradoxes of human conduct and personality, with sympathy as well as understanding."[2]

## Understanding Employees

Like all human beings, employees are a complex set of paradoxes and contradictory characteristics. To make the change effort work, we must learn how to capitalize on positive human qualities, such as trust, idealism, and dedication, and mitigate the impact of those other natural human traits (suspicion, stubbornness, anxiety) that often undermine the change process.

How do we accomplish this formidable task? First, we need to understand our employees by gathering interview data from them. What do they think of their department or organization, both positive and negative? How do they believe its performance can be improved? If they were in charge, what changes would they make? How would these changes affect them and their coworkers? How would they evaluate the leadership of their unit or company? What do they like and dislike about their jobs?

The answers to these and other questions help to determine what's most important to the employees, in which areas they are satisfied and dissatisfied, whether or not they recognize an urgent need for change, and, if so, where they want these changes to occur.

The information-gathering stage is far more critical to any change

2. Harold Bloom, ed., *Modern Critical Interpretations: F. Scott Fitzgerald's "The Great Gatsby"* (New York: Chelsea House, 1986), 39.

effort than leaders or consultants frequently realize. Since the ultimate struggle is for the minds of the employees, those minds must be fully understood at a minimum of two different levels:

1. How the individual's mind works
2. How the perceptual world of the organization or the group works

## How an Individual's Mind Works

Humans are not, by nature, solitary creatures. They do not live alone in caves, solely motivated by their own thoughts and drives. Humans are social animals, they are mammals who form dominance and sexual hierarchies, live mostly in symbolic worlds, and, at least in Western society, are largely dominated by fear and guilt. For almost all humans, there is also a large discrepancy between how they see themselves and how they are seen by others. Almost no one is entirely objective about his or her own actions. What people do, instead, is to develop idealized views of themselves and try to ignore information that contradicts these views. Nevertheless, they often find themselves in a bind between what society expects of them and what they actually feel and want to do.

Suppose a professional basketball player is removed from the game with only a minute left on the clock. He is replaced by someone else, who is instrumental in scoring the winning basket just as the buzzer sounds. How does this player feel after the game? Does he believe that the coach made the right decision in removing him because the other player is better? How many people can be that objective with themselves, even if it is true? What's more, would a team want a player who doesn't think he is the best? This is often called "having a positive attitude." Such an attitude motivates a player to strive for excellence, to be the best he can be, and to maximize his performance on the basketball court.

After the game, the player is interviewed by the media, and a reporter asks him how he feels about being taken out with only a minute to play. If the player is like most people, he probably feels a combination of anger, frustration, denigration, relief, guilt, and maybe, to a lesser extent, some gratification that his team won the game. But what does he tell the reporter? It is probably most advantageous for the player to give a slanted version of the truth. "It was the coach's decision, and I'm glad we won." This is only a half truth, but if the player says anything else, it may prove extremely costly for him. The coach may be angry at him and give him less playing time in future games. His teammates may call him a poor sport who puts his own feelings ahead of the team's needs, and they may pass the ball to him less often. As a result, he might score fewer points, which would not only affect his own sense of accomplishment but also reduce the amount of money he receives in his next contract.

Faced with these consequences, few players would be foolish enough to reveal their true feelings, although they might want to express them. Instead, social norms reinforce a decision to hide these feelings—whether you play on a basketball team or work for a large corporation.

This discussion is designed to demonstrate a few principles that are basic to understanding human nature:

▲ Never accept at face value what people say they feel or believe. Instead, watch what they do; this will give you a much more accurate understanding of their feelings and attitudes. As we said earlier, employees may say that they accept the change process, then do everything in their power to stonewall it.

▲ The consequences of an action have an enormous impact on behavior. What this means is that an organization must reward the type of behavior it wants to promote and sanction that which it wants to discourage.

▲ Human beings are full of contradictions and paradoxes because that is the nature of human social life.

▲ Frequently, the only way to understand another person or group is to use your empathy and intuition and imagine what you would feel in a similar circumstance. Of course, your ability to put yourself in the other person's shoes is affected by how well you really understand yourself. If you are not able to be honest with yourself about how you feel in a situation, you will have severe difficulty understanding another person's feelings.

## How the Perceptual World of the Organization or Group Works

Although the basketball player expressed no negative feelings to the reporter about the coach's decision to take him out of the game, he still feels angry and unappreciated. What happens to these feelings will depend both on how the player deals with them and on how his teammates react. Will they support their coach's decision? Will they support the player? Or will their reactions vary?

There is no objective social reality. One culture values individual competitiveness and another emphasizes teamwork. Individuals find themselves in a microculture every time they are part of a group or an organization. That culture affects how they see themselves and their own actions. You can't see your face directly; you must look in a mirror, and that mirror is the reactions of others. Remember when you were an adolescent and wanted to find out how you looked. You would ask your parents, or your peers—especially members of the opposite sex. We monitor our behavior and attitudes by the way that others deal with us. And we often alter these things, consciously and unconsciously, to gain acceptance, stature, and support from our peers.

Let's consider the basketball player and his teammates again. If his teammates support their coach and respect his judgments, and if they have a strong sense of unity, they may say to the player, "Hey, Joe, shake it off. It's just one game." Frequently, this type of reaction will help the player put his feelings behind him and conform to the rest of the team. But suppose there is a faction whose members dislike the coach and share the player's feeling that the coach is arbitrary in his decisions. They feel alienated from the coach and the other players, like the Outs. Perhaps some of them are high-performance stars, who carry a great deal of influence on the team. If the player becomes part of this group, then they will confirm his feelings. Eventually, this faction may cause so much disruption that the team begins to destroy itself and the coach is fired.

The same thing occurs inside many organizations involved in a change process. The greatest danger occurs if there is a split, with half the high-performance, high-stature employees supporting the process and half opposing it. These informal leaders determine, to a great extent, what others think and feel. Most change efforts flounder because a significant number of these informal leaders resist; they demonize the formal leader, and there is no way he or she can apply enough leverage to get the process moving. When this happens, the formal leader has lost.

## The Importance of Information Gathering

It should now be clear why the information-gathering stage is so important and why accurate information is so difficult to obtain. The five guidelines that follow may prove useful:

1. Never depend on what one individual says. Having multiple sources for the same information is the only way to screen out individual biases.
2. Even if multiple sources yield the same information, it may still not be entirely accurate. Instead, it may reflect only what people think they should say.
3. Therefore, it's important to know how the culture works—what it rewards and what it sanctions.
4. Some people's opinions will be far more useful than others'. Talk to the formal and informal leaders and find out their attitudes.
5. Employ outside information sources, such as consultants and independent surveys. They tend to be far less biased.

## *Making Change Work*

Information creates the platform from which to mount a dynamic social process to produce change. The social process is designed to build upon everything that might advance the change effort. For example, the process might try to capitalize on the positive feelings that employees have expressed about their organization or the suggestions they have offered to improve their jobs. The social process also tries to mitigate anything that may stand in the way of change, such as a suspicion of top management among employees or their fear that they cannot master the skills they need to succeed in a new culture.

Dynamic social processes come in all shapes and sizes. No two change processes ever start the same way, nor does their ultimate success depend on the same things. Individual circumstances vary. For example, organization A may be clearly failing, while organization B may appear healthy. As a result, the employees in organization A may accept the necessity for change much more readily, and it may need to occur much more rapidly. Organization B may have a charismatic leader—one who has come up through the ranks, has earned the respect of employees, and can direct the change process effectively. Organization A, on the other hand, may have a new CEO—one who has a dynamic vision for change but is an unknown quantity to employees and thus is less likely to be trusted by them. Information gathering among employees may also reveal that their morale is extremely low and that they have lost faith in the ability of their organization to chart a successful course into the future. These are some of the circumstances that must be taken into consideration as a social process to produce change is designed. There is no right or wrong process; there are only processes that are dictated by the situation that exists inside a specific organization. Let us give you an example.

Several years ago, a company was formed from the merger of two large communications firms. Unfortunately, their disparate cultures were not fully integrated, and the employees had never learned to regard each other as members of the same organization. Without strong internal cohesion, the company was ill prepared to deal with the heavy competition it confronted in the marketplace. New product development cycles were too long, shipments to customers were repeatedly behind schedule, overhead costs were escalating, and several rounds of layoffs had decimated key departments. One of these was the sales department, where managers had been stunned by the unexpected announcement that their popular boss had just been fired because she had failed to improve operations.

The new boss, a short, outspoken, middle-aged executive, had been very successful running other departments in the organization, but he recognized that sales might prove to be an extremely difficult challenge. The employees were demoralized, suspicious of top management, whom they saw as the cause of all their problems, and resentful toward their new department head; moreover, the CEO expected him to turn around the operation not in the two to three years that turnarounds generally require, but in six to nine months.

While this manager had a clear vision of what he wanted to accomplish, the problem was how to get the employees to buy into it. He not only wanted them to accept change, he also hoped to transform the culture of the department so that employees would feel empowered to initiate more change—something they had never done before. He realized that this was the only type of culture that could respond to the market quickly enough. It was a tall order, requiring a social process that included several key elements:

▲ A group experience to help rebuild morale
▲ A program to unlock the individual energy of each manager and supervisor
▲ The restoration of hope among employees in the future of their organization
▲ A disconfirmation of the old ways of doing things
▲ A new vision

## *Initiating the Change Process*

With the help of an outside consulting team, the new manager developed two training programs based on these elements. Conducted several months apart, they were aimed at all managers and supervisors in the department. He decided not to start the first seminar with his new vision (one of the traditional starting points for change efforts). Interview data showed that the managers and supervisors were already feeling overwhelmed by all the events occurring inside their organization, and many of them were angry that their old boss had been replaced. If the new boss were to stand up and present his vision, it would only make matters worse. Instead, the training program was to focus on improving the employees' morale and self-esteem, helping them bond with their new leader, opening them up to change, and enabling them to adapt to it.

The manager introduced the program by expressing his hope that it would prove helpful to all of the participants. Then, as the first exercise of the morning, they were asked to consider the major environmental factors that were affecting their business. They broke up into small groups, each looking at a single factor and exploring its impact on the company, their department, and themselves. Afterward, they reconvened as a whole group and shared their information. This enabled everyone to realize that change was affecting all of them—it was affecting their entire organization and, indeed, their whole industry. Once they had accepted this fact, it was extremely difficult to blame someone else for the problems that were besetting them.

Too often, as Peter Senge points out in *The Fifth Discipline,* employees tend to see the cause of a problem as something outside their own control—somebody in the next department or at the next higher management level is the cause. Employees are content to concentrate on their own narrow area, and if things go wrong, they may try to blame someone else. "It's their fault," they say. "It's not my problem." But it is! Every department is part of a single process, and everyone must work together to improve the entire operation so that all the gears will begin meshing properly again.

As the participants in the seminar began to see their problems in a broader context, most of them also recognized not only that change was essential, but that they had to lead it and persuade other employees to follow them. The only way that managers and supervisors would feel comfortable with change was to be part of an entire organization that was embracing the change process. "You need to *lead* people into battle," one of them said. "It's impossible to *manage* people into battle." But how were they going to become leaders? By developing leadership skills. While it may seem somewhat paradoxical for an individual to embrace personal development for the sake of his or her organization, this is often an essential prerequisite for change.

Once the participants became more comfortable discussing the magnitude of these problems and sharing their feelings about the impact of these problems on all of them, they were asked to turn their attention inward to more personal issues. Everyone considered two questions:

1. What has been changing for you personally and professionally?
2. What is the impact of these changes on you and your family?

This gave everyone an opportunity to talk about the issues affecting their morale. It was also a clear signal from their new leader that he was concerned about the problems that affected them as individuals.

Next, the participants were asked to examine their leadership styles. They were instructed to evaluate their own abilities in areas such as delegating or team building and to predict how their subordinates would rate them. Then they were given data collected from their subordinates. There was often a large discrepancy between the scores the participants gave themselves and the much lower scores that their subordinates gave them.

These data helped the participants to disconnect from their old leadership styles and begin to open themselves up to the necessity for change.

## Life Charts

To help the participants understand some of the personal problems that might have been standing in the way of their becoming better leaders, they were taught how to make their own life charts. A life chart is a graphic depiction of your life from the earliest days until the present, showing who you are and what's really important to you. Constructing a life chart takes about forty minutes, and participants are asked to diagram their life according to four dimensions: *relationships*—the quality of their relationships with friends, family, and associates; *achievement*—important accomplishments, like college honors, promotions at work, or outstanding projects; *power*—positions held in school, on the job, or in the community; and *satisfaction*—which usually reflects the other three dimensions, and which answers the question "How content am I?" at any given point in life.

Let's look at the life chart of a manager (Figure 4-1). Jim is a forty-nine-year-old senior editor in a major publishing firm. He had grown up in an Eastern suburb, where his mother worked as a librarian and his father owned a clothing store. Jim never made many friends when he was a boy, preferring the company of his parents. He was especially close to his father, a very demanding individual who never handed out praise for Jim's schoolwork without also telling him that it could still stand improvement. His father called it "constructive criticism," but it left Jim always feeling inadequate.

Jim's performance in elementary school was above average, and he was even elected class president, but his life took an abrupt change for the worse in junior high when his parents moved him to a prestigious private school. He simply couldn't keep up with the work, and he never fit in with the other students. Eventually, Jim's father transferred him to another school, where his performance improved tremendously. Jim threw himself into the work, studying five and six hours a day and eventually winning a scholarship to a prestigious college. Although he was elected president of his fraternity, Jim never felt very close to any of the other students. Recalling a particularly tough decision that faced him during his term as president, Jim explained that he didn't seek the advice of any of his peers, but immediately telephoned his father.

Following graduation, Jim entered the navy for a three-year term; during that time, his father died.

This was a low point in Jim's life; indeed, it was several years before his satisfaction curve regained the level it held during his childhood.

**Figure 4-1. Life chart for a senior editor.**

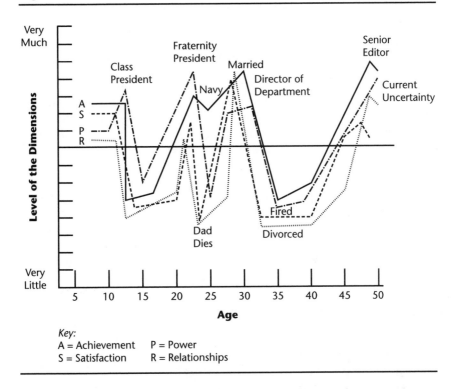

<br />

After his discharge from the navy, Jim married a woman whom he met in graduate school, but their marriage never seemed to satisfy either of them, and a few years later they were divorced. This marked another extremely low point for Jim.

Jim continued to devote himself to publishing, becoming director of his department—the youngest in the firm's history. He was a workaholic and demanded nothing less from his subordinates. Unfortunately, this didn't protect him when the firm was sold to a much larger company. Jim couldn't get along with his new boss, and he was abruptly fired. For the next several years, he held a number of different jobs before coming to his current firm, where he has risen steadily to his present position. Now merger talks are in the air, and they're creating a new atmosphere of uncertainty.

Jim's life chart shows that while he is very achievement-oriented and derives high satisfaction from his accomplishments, he has a problem maintaining relationships, which began in childhood. And this is reflected in the way he managed his staff, who reported that they rarely seemed to satisfy his exacting standards. Thus, while Jim may have been a brilliant editor, he was a poor leader—a critical skill for anyone in his position.

## Change the Individual/Change the Organization

The participants in the training seminar broke into small groups and constructed life charts like the example we just showed you. This was the first time that most of them had ever delved so deeply into their past lives, and it proved to be a highly emotional experience. Each participant achieved not only a more profound insight into himself or herself, but a better understanding of the forces that motivate all human beings—both of which are critically important to becoming a better manager. Sharing the results with their group enabled every participant to broaden his or her perspective even further, while at the same time building an atmosphere of camaraderie and teamwork that often results from the exchange of such personal information. The sense of belonging to a group also helped the participants deal more effectively with the stress created by the current conditions in their department.

As a final step in the seminar, people worked in small groups to determine what they needed to do to solve their personal problems, deal with stress, and become better leaders. Each person put together a three-month plan to improve his or her life and management style in the department, with specific milestones and a verbal commitment to report progress to the other members of the group.

Almost all the managers kept this commitment. The seminar had significantly boosted their morale by enabling them to concentrate on a course of action that not only improved their personal lives but benefited their organization, as well.

This seminar employed a successful leverage point: It focused on each participant's human needs and linked them to the situation in the department. Those needs, of course, will not be the same in every organization, and so the leverage points will inevitably be different. But by gathering data about the people in an organization, it is possible to begin to understand their concerns; and when these concerns are addressed to the extent possible, the change process can be started.

The leverage is created by determining not only the issues on which to focus but the order in which to present them. This also varies with the situation. Here the training seminar started with a consideration of external events affecting the sales department; then it went to personal issues; next to leadership style; then back to personal issues with the life charts; and finally to an action plan for change.

Once they began to see their personal lives in a new perspective, the participants in the seminar found it easier to disconnect from an ineffectual management style and open themselves up to initiating change in their department. What's more, they also developed a much closer bond with their new leader, to whom they felt grateful for arranging this seminar and helping them deal with important personal issues. He had reached into their hearts.

As a result, three months later at a second workshop, when the manager presented his new vision for the sales department and his plan for executing it, all the participants enthusiastically supported him. That support would not have been given without a carefully designed process for the second workshop (which is more appropriately discussed in Chapter 6.) With a vision and a strategy for addressing the organizational issues inside the department, a process of self-perpetuating change began.

▲ ▲ ▲ ▲

As we have explained in this chapter, an understanding of human nature lies at the center of any successful change process. Leaders must be able to look inside the minds of their employees and recognize what motivates them. They must also realize that humans are motivated not only by rational considerations, but by irrational ones as well. Therefore, an effective leader knows how to win the battle for their hearts. Since human beings are social animals and organizations are social settings, leaders must also realize that group dynamics play a key role in influencing employee attitudes and actions. Information about all of these factors—accurate information readily available before a change process is initiated—is critical if leaders are to produce the change that they desire.

# 5

# The Uses of Power: Patterns of Failure and Success

On September 3, 1919, President Woodrow Wilson, looking haggard and already severely weakened by exhaustion, boarded a train for a grueling 10,000-mile whistle-stop tour across the country. It was a last desperate attempt to save the League of Nations.

This was an astounding turn of events for a man who, a scant nine months earlier, had been hailed as the savior of the world. Arriving in Brest the previous December, he had been greeted by crowds of children lining the streets, waving American flags and holding signs that read "Hail the Champion of the Rights of Man," "Honor and Welcome to the Founder of the Society of Nations." In Paris, a far more tumultuous reception awaited him. "Vive Wilson," the crowds shouted as he rode down the Champs-Élysées accompanied by French President Raymond Poincaré. When their entourage emerged through the Arc de Triomphe, it passed under a huge banner that proclaimed "Honor to Wilson the Just."

"From the very beginning of this war," the president told a group of assembled notables later that day, "the thoughts of the people of America turned toward something higher than the mere spoils of war. Their thought was directed toward the establishment of the eternal principles of right and justice." It was to be a peace like no other before it, a peace without victory following a cataclysmic war that had claimed an entire generation of young men. And the foundations of international security would be Wilson's immortal Fourteen Points—an idealistic framework that included the League of Nations.

Unfortunately, Wilson's idealism was no match for the pugnacious spirit he encountered among the other Allied leaders. Prime Minister Da-

68

vid Lloyd George of England, for example, had just won reelection on a platform that called on the Germans to be treated as a vanquished nation and pay "every last farthing" for the cost of the war. And Georges Clemenceau, the premier of France, had received a standing ovation in the Chamber of Deputies when he openly scoffed at the league.

"Everyone seems to be trying to further their own interests," one of Wilson's associates wrote sadly. "It is a selfish bunch."[1]

Indeed, this "bunch" proved too powerful for Wilson. The stress of the peace conference caused the president to visibly age almost overnight and set one side of his face twitching uncontrollably. In its final form, the Treaty of Versailles violated many of Wilson's sacred Fourteen Points and imposed a crushing burden of reparations on Germany. But at least he had managed to save the League of Nations.

When the president arrived home, he was in no mood to fight still another battle with a recalcitrant Senate over the confirmation of the treaty and acceptance of his precious league. But that was exactly what now confronted him. Although the Republicans had won control of the Congress in the election of 1918, Wilson had refused to include any of their leaders as part of the American peace delegation to Paris. The Republican leaders were miffed, and many of them also harbored genuine misgivings about the league, especially Article X, which committed America to defend European nations in case of invasion. Not only did they fail to share Wilson's noble sense of idealism when it came to preserving international peace, they also feared that if he won a great victory on the world stage, it might catapult him into a third term as president.

Leading the fight against ratification was the wily Senate majority leader, Henry Cabot Lodge. Wilson and Lodge detested each other, but the senator knew that if he led a direct frontal assault on the League, he would be defeated because Wilson was far too popular throughout the country. Instead, he proposed to debate the league to death with a series of reservations that would reduce its effectiveness. But would this strategy work?

"Suppose the President accepts the treaty with your reservations," one of his colleagues asked him. "Then we are in the league, and once in, our reservations become purely fictional."

Lodge looked at him. "You do not take into consideration the hatred that Woodrow Wilson has for me personally. Never under any set of circumstances in this world could he be induced to accept a treaty with Lodge reservations appended to it."[2]

1. Gene Smith, *When the Cheering Stopped: The Last Years of Woodrow Wilson* (New York: Morrow, 1964).
2. James Watson, *As I Knew Them: Memoirs of James E. Watson* (Indianapolis: Bobbs-Merrill, 1936).

And Lodge was right. Instead, the president pushed harder and harder to have the Senate accept the treaty as written. And the more he lobbied, the more stubborn his opposition became. Finally, Wilson was forced to take his case directly to the people.

Speaking first in Columbus, Ohio, he told the cheering crowd that only the league could prevent another world war. And from the back of the presidential train in Richmond, Indiana, he exhorted: "What difference does party make when mankind is involved?"

As the train proceeded on to St. Louis, Omaha, and Sioux Falls, the heat was excruciating and the president was visibly weakening. But he refused to stop, his mission seemed far too important. As he told the crowds in Bismarck, "The whole world is waiting on us."

That fall, however, other events seemed far more worrisome to many Americans than the fate of the league. A series of strikes was crippling the country, and people wondered why the president had not been focusing his attention on this problem. In addition, the nation was sinking into an economic slump that would cost thousands of workers their jobs. But as the presidential train sped westward, Wilson was consumed by his fight for the league—his league—and in speech after speech at Spokane, San Francisco, Los Angeles, San Diego he urged the crowds to join him on his righteous crusade.

Finally the president headed eastward and home. He looked gaunt and exhausted—dangerously so, some of his aides believed. Stopping in Pueblo, Colorado, Wilson seemed to stumble as he mounted the platform, then, unaccountably, he suddenly stopped midsentence during his speech and momentarily appeared unable to continue. That night the president complained that he could not sleep and felt extremely ill. By the next morning, as the train approached Wichita, it was clear that his condition had grown more serious. Indeed, Wilson had suffered a thrombosis of the brain—the left side of his face sagged, and his left arm and leg were paralyzed.

The rest of the tour was canceled. The president never recovered his health. And America never joined the League of Nations because Wilson and the Republicans in the United States Senate refused to compromise.

The tragic drama of Woodrow Wilson and the struggle for the League of Nations demonstrates some of the key elements of the change process, whether it occurs in the giant arena of international diplomacy or within the paneled boardroom of a major corporation. Change is generally precipitated by a serious crisis—World War I, for example, or a severe downturn in a company's economic performance—that destabilizes the situation and shakes the very foundation of accepted practices. A leader may then appear with a vision of how to deal with this crisis, clothed in high-sounding, idealistic rhetoric—Wilson's Fourteen Points or a CEO's clarion call to make every business in a company's portfolio number one or number two in its field. How can anyone disagree with such noble goals? But people do—not openly, perhaps, but behind those heavy doors that guard the corridors of power. The naysayers may simply have an honest difference of opinion, or they may be afraid of change, or perhaps they detest the leader who's spearheading the change process. The more the leader pushes, the harder they resist. The raw exercise of power often produces gridlock, whether it's in the U.S. government or a *Fortune* 500 company. A leader must learn to rely on more subtle and indirect methods of influence, but these require a thorough knowledge of human nature (which Wilson obviously lacked).

Eventually, a leader may try to sidestep the stubborn opposition by appealing to the rest of her or his constituency, just as Wilson did. But here again, success will depend on a clear recognition of constituents' concerns and interests as well as the proper application of power and influence. The goal is to create a critical mass of support that will make the change process irreversible, but this usually means waging hundreds and hundreds of battles for the hearts of would-be supporters over a lengthy period of time. For Woodrow Wilson, time simply ran out.

Wilson's experience with the league demonstrates how easy it is for a gifted leader to fatally misunderstand human nature and fail to apply power effectively. As a result, an idealistic, high-minded change process, designed to move America onto the world stage, was postponed for an entire generation.

## An Example of Power

Most managers are reluctant to talk about the use of power, especially in this age of employee empowerment. Power conjures up images of deals made in back rooms, of agreements reached under the table, of *politics*. And what word could be as dirty as *politics*—except, of course, *power*. And yet power, properly applied, is exactly what it takes to make the change process work.

At General Electric, Welch used his power to manufacture a crisis that became the catalyst for change. Once the transformation began, he kept it running by controlling some of the traditional power sources of any organization. As Noel Tichy and Stratford Sherman point out in *Control Your Destiny or Someone Else Will,* Welch dominated the internal media through articles and speeches articulating his vision for the company. He turned the corporate structure on its head, eliminating the authority of the central staffers who had been the arbiters of every planning and financial decision made by the business managers and vesting far more of this power in the managers themselves, decentralizing the entire organization and enabling each business to respond more rapidly to events in the marketplace. Of course, Welch still held the purse strings, and with this power he forced his managers—sometimes brutally—to face up to the painful downsizing and costcutting necessary to make their operations more competitive.

By the end of 1984, having sold off 117 business units, Welch had literally dismantled the old General Electric. While the change process now seemed irreversible, there was still enormous resistance among his managers. One way the CEO decided to deal with this problem was by utilizing Crotonville, the GE management training center, as an instrument to fashion a new breed of manager. And he put Tichy to work creating a curriculum that would help do the job. Crotonville played a critical role in winning the battle for the hearts and minds of the company's managers. This has been a multifaceted process, taking many years to accomplish, and it has transformed the entire culture at GE.

Anyone who has led a department or organization knows how difficult it is to produce large-scale change. The principal goal of the change process is to produce alignment among the employees behind a new corporate direction, new cultural values, new methods of operating. It is one thing for a CEO to say that he or she is for empowerment, or quality, or internationalization; it is quite another to align the employees behind these objectives. Alignment means that top managers and their subordinates have embraced the company's new direction in their hearts and minds—that their behavior is consistent with the new cultural values, not because they are afraid of what the leader will do to them if they don't go along, but because they actually believe in the change process that is occurring inside their organization. This means that a CEO must have a clear understanding of human nature, as we explained in the preceding chapter. It also requires a skillful use of power.

## Types of Power

In the modern organization, *power* refers to the various methods available to a leader to achieve alignment. Remember, the ultimate goal of power in producing organizational change is alignment, nothing less.

### Coercive Power

The ultimate authority of the leader is the ability to fire subordinates. The threat of coercive power may be enough to make employees sit up and listen to a leader, but it is completely insufficient to produce alignment. Although subordinates do not want to be fired, they will frequently resist a CEO's authority—usually doing it covertly. Parents often encounter the same situation with their children. "Don't fight with your brother," a parent says as he separates his two young sons, "or I'll punish you." While the parent is standing in front of them, the children will obey because they fear the consequences. But a short time later, when the parent has gone, his children may resume fighting. Coercive power often produces covert defiance and resistance among individuals in a subordinate position—which is the exact opposite of alignment.

## Formal Power

Sometimes authority comes with an individual's role. The CEO, for example, has the formal power to change corporate structures, create new compensation systems, and allocate resources differently. All of these may be essential elements of a corporate transformation process. By changing the compensation system, for instance, managers can be induced to function as team players. But, by itself, formal power is not sufficient to produce alignment. Managers may resent what they're being asked to do, unless they can be shown that it will serve their interests and produce impressive results.

## Expert Power

Expert power is often a necessary ingredient in the alignment process. Suppose, for example, that after suffering for several days with a cough and a fever, a man decides to visit his doctor. The doctor takes a chest x-ray and says that the man has pneumonia. She tells the patient to take a regimen of pills and he will feel better. The patient complies with the doctor's orders because he regards her as an expert. He believes that she knows something that he doesn't, and he is willing to be influenced and led by her. A social contract forms in which the patient internalizes the doctor's explanation of his illness and her instructions for how to get better, his anxiety is relieved, and he is given some pills that will help him. The doctor has influenced the patient's heart and mind, as well as his actions. Effective leaders can have a similar impact on subordinates who believe that they possess an expertise, often based on such things as a track record of past success, that enables them to see the world more clearly and understand problems more accurately than anyone else in an organization. This is usually an important element in achieving alignment.

## Moral Power

There is an organizational high ground that leaders often try to seize by cloaking their directives in the inspirational language of a vision statement or business imperative. "Satisfying the customer" or "becoming the best in our business" or "rescuing the company from impending disaster" can serve as persuasive rhetoric that helps create alignment among employees. Of course, for a vision to be most effective, a leader must embody its tenets. That is, he or she must set the moral example. It's no good to preach product quality when employees see that what's really being rewarded is the number of products that roll off the assembly line each day.

## Referent Power

Sometimes power derives from the people who endorse a leader and his or her methods. For example, suppose you work for a volunteer group that is trying to assist the homeless. One of your colleagues suggests that an effective method of fund raising would be to hold a celebrity dinner. Since she is personally acquainted with many of the celebrities who would be invited, you agree that she should direct the fund-raising event. You are willing to be influenced and led by her because she is accepted by a group of people whom you value and respect.

## Relationship Power

All of us make use of relationship power from time to time without even thinking about it. "Please do it for me," we say to our friends. Conversely, we will put ourselves out for someone else whom we like or whom we want to like us. Relationship power depends on such attributes as an individual's charm, charisma, sense of humor, and positive reputation among colleagues.

▲  ▲  ▲  ▲

The subtler forms of power—relationship, referent, moral, and expert—work on the hearts and minds of employees, and therefore they are the most effective at achieving alignment. But it often takes far more to influence employees to support a change process. Suppose, for example, a new CEO joins your company. He seems to be a generally likable fellow (relationship power). Your organization is in trouble, and the CEO, who has worked in the industry for many years, has saved another company that was on the brink of disaster (expert power). Recently, he appeared on the cover of *Fortune* magazine, which praised his work (referent power). The CEO walks into your office one morning and discusses his vision for transforming the organization. Then, at the end of the conference, he asks for your support.

Will you support him? What if it means taking on some new responsibilities and risking the possibility of failing? Or giving up some of your autonomy? Or lowering your status in the organization? Perhaps you'll decide to give the appearance of supporting the CEO, while taking a "wait and see" attitude. Perhaps you'll even decide to work covertly to oppose him. Most likely, you'll make up some justification for taking this action that hides the true reason (your own self-interest) even from yourself. "The CEO's methods may have worked somewhere else," you'll say, "but he doesn't understand our organization." No matter how much power a CEO may possess, unless you believe that he or she understands you and your needs and advocates your interests, you probably won't go along. That's the way human nature works.

As we discussed in the preceding chapter, a leader who thoroughly understands human nature can channel it to support the change process. A leader can employ power in the same way. This means a skillful use of the subtler forms of power as a way of overcoming resistance and procuring alignment. It means knowing when to use formal power and coercive power. But, just as important, it involves an understanding of power relationships and how to utilize them in support of change.

## Powergrams

Power flows between human beings along specific channels. The flow depends on the relationship between the individuals and the amount of power that the receiver perceives the sender to possess. To understand power relationships, it helps to use diagrams as an effective method of making the concepts visible and clear. Figure 5-1 shows some of the symbols used in powergrams.

Figure 5-2 shows a situation that might exist on a top management team. A has become the new CEO of the company. He has been successful in developing a good relationship with the vice president of sales (B), who endorses the changes in the organization that the CEO wants to make and supports his authority. However, the vice president of manufacturing (C) distrusts the new CEO and is covertly trying to undermine him. Under these circumstances, what are the CEO's options?

1. He can keep talking to C and hope to win him over. While the manufacturing vice president may say that he supports his boss,

## Figure 5-1. Symbols used in powergrams.

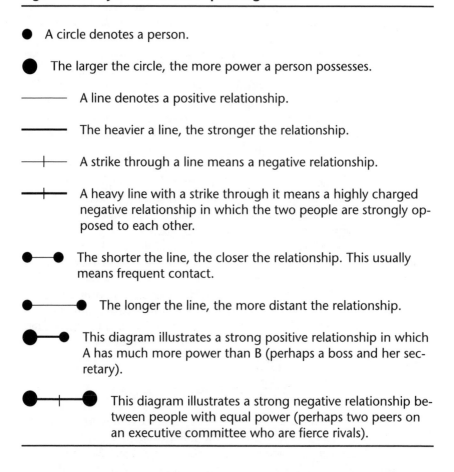

● A circle denotes a person.

● The larger the circle, the more power a person possesses.

——— A line denotes a positive relationship.

—— The heavier a line, the stronger the relationship.

—|— A strike through a line means a negative relationship.

—|— A heavy line with a strike through it means a highly charged negative relationship in which the two people are strongly opposed to each other.

●—● The shorter the line, the closer the relationship. This usually means frequent contact.

●———● The longer the line, the more distant the relationship.

●—● This diagram illustrates a strong positive relationship in which A has much more power than B (perhaps a boss and her secretary).

●—|—● This diagram illustrates a strong negative relationship between people with equal power (perhaps two peers on an executive committee who are fierce rivals).

chances are that their relationship will worsen. C may feel that the CEO is only trying to put him on the spot.

2. He can use his formal power and order C to carry out his directives. But this will only reinforce C's resistance.
3. He can fire C.

However, the diagram points out an additional alternative. The CEO can go to the vice president of sales, with whom he has a good relationship and who, in turn, has a positive rapport with his colleague, the vice president for manufacturing. He can discuss C's resistance and ask B to talk with C and persuade him to support the change process. This approach does not always prove effective, but it has a much better chance of success

**Figure 5-2. Powergram of possible relationships on a top management team.**

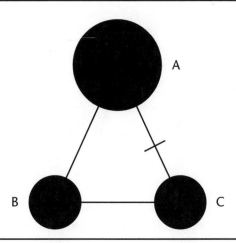

**Figure 5-3. Powergram showing more complicated relationships.**

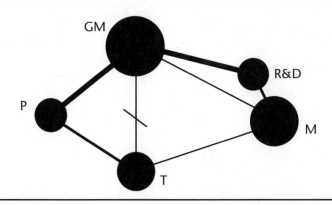

than the other three options. The use of the powergram helps to clarify the relationships among individuals and show how power can be used most effectively.

Let's look at a little more complicated example (Figure 5-3), the relationships between Bob Jeffries, the general manager of a manufacturing plant, and several of his subordinates. Jeffries has a very good relationship with the purchasing manager, Harold Marino, whom he hired for a

**Figure 5-4. Powergram of a cohesive group.**

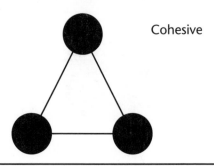

Cohesive

similar position when he ran another plant. It's quite a different story with the director of transportation, Sheila Carlson, however. Sheila has expressed serious skepticism about Bob's leadership style ever since he came to the plant three months ago. Nevertheless, Sheila and Harold have a good relationship, so if Bob can convince Harold, he may be able to win over a reluctant Sheila.

The GM had never worked with Earl Hilton, his manufacturing boss, before coming to this plant, so the two of them are still getting comfortable with each other. However, Bob does have a close relationship with Lanford Harris, director of R&D. When Bob had a staff job at corporate headquarters, he was instrumental in helping Lanford obtain additional funding for his department, and since that time they have regularly kept in touch with each other. Lanford and Earl Hilton play golf every weekend, so Bob Jeffries can use his relationship with Harris to influence Hilton.

## *Power in Groups*

Whenever people work together, they form groups. These may be formal groups, like a manufacturing department, or informal ones. Relationships among members of the group may be positive or negative. There will be specific channels of influence, communication, and power, and norms (patterns) that govern the group's operations. (We'll use three-person groups for simplicity in this discussion, but the same structures apply no matter how large the group may be.)

In a cohesive group, for example, there are positive relationships among all the members (Figure 5-4). Each member might have the same amount of power (e.g., a self-directed work team with a leader/coach), or the manager might have more power than subordinates. When all the group members arrive at their job every day, they come with specific expectations of what each of their roles should be, the quality of work they should produce, the number of hours they should put in, and how they should be compensated for their performance.

Suppose the group leader is now informed by a superior that these expectations must change as part of a corporate reorganization. The team will be expected to undertake additional responsibilities, requiring that each member learn new skills, but no one will be paid any more money. How will the leader react?

Perhaps she willingly accepts the necessity for these changes, especially if the organization seems threatened by an impending crisis, and persuades the other members of her team to go along with them. But she might also decide to resist the change process, the way managers do every day. Inside a cohesive group, the influence process works in both directions. The leader can persuade the other group members to support a new initiative, but they, in turn, can influence her to resist it. Perhaps she and her coworkers have made an enormous effort to build the cohesiveness of their team; they trust one another, and together they have achieved new performance standards in their department. Suppose the other team members are opposed to making any change. The leader may fear that if she supports the changes, she will upset the relationship with her coworkers, who may then try to distance themselves from her. And her relationship with her coworkers may mean more to her than the perceived value of whatever change is being advocated.

The advantage of a cohesive team is that it simplifies the transformation process. Change the leader and you almost always change the team. The disadvantage is that if you fail to change the leader, then the team will stably resist the transformation process.

Another kind of group is a fragmented one (Figure 5-5). Suppose a leader is creating a new work team. At the outset, there is no cohesion, and it is up to the team leader to build it.

The advantage of a fragmented team is that it is unstable. Bonds will eventually form, and the team will find direction. But when the team is still fragmented, the leader has an enormous opportunity to influence how these bonds will be created and what direction the team will follow. This is one of the reasons that change can often be produced by restructuring. When new departments are created, they operate like fragmented groups. A skillful leader who understands human nature and knows how to use influence can create an extremely cohesive group that will follow her or him. Frequently the leader is invested with more power than the other team members, which becomes an additional tool for team building. Many people find power attractive and are predisposed to conform

**Figure 5-5. Powergram of a fragmented group.**

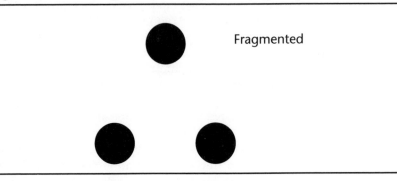

Fragmented

**Figure 5-6. Powergram of an antinorm group.**

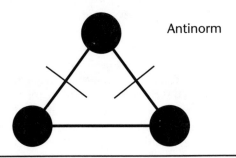

Antinorm

to the wishes of anyone who has it. Consider what happens when a new president comes to Washington or a new CEO is selected to occupy the corner office.

However, an unskilled leader can just as easily misuse power to create what we call an *antinorm* group (Figure 5-6). In this type of group, the subordinates join together and resist the leader. They become the classic Outs described by Kerwyn Smith in *Groups in Conflict*. They resent the leader (the Elite), distrust his motives, and eventually oppose each of his initiatives simply because he is the one proposing it. The leader, in turn, develops the same attitude toward them. This is the situation that developed between Wilson and Lodge and his Republican colleagues in the struggle over the League of Nations.

Antinorm groups are usually very stable and highly resistant to a leader and his or her goals and vision of change. And the more power a leader exerts, the more resistant these groups become. Take the relationship between union and management that may exist inside a plant.

Management wants to make certain changes in the work rules. If an atmosphere of mistrust exists, the union may suspect management's motives, no matter what they may be, and perceive that power is being used unfairly. The union resists the change; management pushes harder, forcing the union to react. Union members draw together and strike. The strike may bring them closer together, since they are dependent on one another for survival. And their resistance grows even stronger.

There are several strategies for dealing with an antinorm group. The first is to coopt its leaders. By focusing attention on what will influence them, the CEO can often draw the leaders into a closer relationship. Special favors and opportunities for additional power may prove especially effective. If the perceptions of the union leaders and the CEO have become distorted, perhaps intermediaries (such as outside consultants) can be found who will help reopen the channels of communication.

A second approach is to break up the antinorm group. This will produce a fragmented group, providing a unique opportunity for the leader to establish new bonds with its members and set a new direction.

## A Difficult Dilemma

How to use power effectively to produce change is one of the most difficult dilemmas facing the leaders of modern organizations. While formal power and coercive power may be necessary to initiate the change process and deal with resistance, if they are used too often or inappropriately, they only produce more resistance—that is, stronger antinorm groups. Subtler forms of power (relationship, expert, etc.) may prove more effective in creating alignment. It may also be possible to coopt the leaders of the opposition. If this doesn't work, replacing the leaders and restructuring may be necessary, creating a fragmented group and allowing the CEO to begin all over again to establish new channels of influence based on his or her understanding of human nature.

Another approach is to play the top and the bottom against those in between. The CEO has the power at the top. Generally, there is a constituency at the bottom that wants more direct power and influence. These employees will attach themselves to the leader, if he or she courts them. Together, they can often neutralize the power of those managers in the middle who may be resisting change.

The health commissioner in a large metropolitan area wanted to reorganize her department to improve the delivery of services to city residents. But she feared that some of the division chiefs who reported to her might try to stonewall her efforts. These old-timers and their direct reports firmly believed that their way of doing things was the best way for everyone. So she decided to go around them. She had worked with several of the chiefs' first- and second-level subordinates on various projects in the past, and she knew that they recognized the need for change. The commissioner plucked these people out from under the noses of their bosses and made them leaders of new cross-functional teams that were charged with restructuring the department. What the commissioner had done was to change the power structure of her department: She removed power from her division chiefs and invested it in the leaders of these cross-functional teams. The teams' mission was to improve services to city residents, and how could the chiefs openly appear to oppose such a noble goal? They had to accept it. And to make life easier for them, the commissioner let it be known that all of the changes in their departments were accomplished under their direction. She had successfully created a rock and a hard place and squeezed the chiefs in between them. Most took early retirement after the teams had reorganized the department.

## *Using Power Effectively*

There are several key guidelines governing the use of power to produce change in an organization. They are:

▲ *Destabilize the situation.* This may have already occurred as the result of a crisis, like the economic problems that gripped the American automobile companies in the early 1980s. If it has not, the leader may create a crisis. Other ways to destabilize conditions are to reshape the structure of the organization, as the city health commissioner did, or to hire a change agent who starts replacing many of the top managers and begins charting a new course for the corporation.

▲ *Develop a vision and articulate it with high-sounding rhetoric.* Use phrases like "satisfying our customers" or "serving the needs of our citizens." Don't be surprised, however, if many employees resist, no matter how noble the goals may appear.

▲ *Try to defuse resistance.* This may be extremely difficult because there are so many reasons for employees to oppose change. The leader must be skilled at using the subtler forms of power wherever possible, exploiting channels of influence, and coopting the opposition. Restructuring and creating fragmented groups may afford an opportunity to set a new direction, and establishing alliances with employees at lower levels of the organization may prove useful in overcoming the opposition of managers in between.

▲ *Don't overlook human nature.* Information gathering can enable a leader to understand the needs and self-interest of employees. Only by using power to satisfy some of these needs is it possible to create alignment with the change process.

▲ *Use power to control the sequence of events.* The leader can determine how a change process begins. Does it start with the announcement of a vision statement? Or by helping managers deal with their stress? What happens second, third, etc.? Frequently, the order of events is critically important. Beginning at the wrong place may simply alienate subordinates and fatally undermine the change process almost before it begins.

▲ *Set a process in motion that becomes self-perpetuating.* This often proves to be the most difficult part of the change effort. Leaders are necessary at every level of the organization to champion the transformation process. These individuals and their subordinates frequently need to be trained in the skills necessary to carry out the corporate revolution. And that revolution also requires a new cultural milieu to nurture and support it. Culture operates essentially at the emotional level, and here the change process can face especially tough obstacles as it tries to win over corporate employees. But if this battle is won, and cohesive groups coalesce around the values and goals of the revolution, the transformation can become irreversible.

## Using Power to Produce Change

Each of the guidelines just described played an important role in facilitating change at a prominent financial services firm. The firm's business was concentrated in two primary areas: providing resource data, software, and advice to asset managers in banks and foundations, and selling investment products, such as mutual funds, to individuals and institutions. Although the firm had become a recognized leader in the first area, that market was becoming saturated, and some clients had already developed the capability of generating the data they needed on their own. A crisis was looming on the horizon and some action would have to be taken to deal with it.

Fortunately, the CEO (a highly competitive man who had been a champion tennis player in college) seemed to have anticipated this problem and even begun shaping a new vision to guide the company in a different direction. This involved restructuring the organization around cross-functional teams, each focused on a major customer segment, and providing it with both data and financial products. However, when he tried to convince his senior vice presidents of the necessity for this type of change, he encountered mixed reactions.

In charge of the area providing resource data and advice was a tall, professorial-looking vice president who had worked for the firm since its inception. He was a very likable man who engendered strong loyalty among his top managers.

They and their field representatives regarded themselves as consultants, not salespeople, and the notion that they should be asked to sell mutual funds to some of their clients appalled them. Nevertheless, they also recognized that their market was becoming saturated. They were logging more and more miles to do the same amount of business as they had done two years earlier, or in many cases even less. Most of these people regarded themselves as "Lone Rangers" who operated completely independent of the company, their primary relationships being with the customers. Indeed, they believed that the company was doing little or nothing to support them.

The CEO spent several months trying to persuade his reluctant vice president that his consultants would have to become sales representatives. When the man continued to resist, he was abruptly fired. If the CEO had tried to take over direct control of the department or appoint a new vice president, he might have created an antinorm group among the consultants. Since they seemed to have little or no loyalty to the organization, they might also decide to resign, taking their clients with them.

Instead, the firm's training department developed a program for these employees with three goals:

1. Strengthen their commitment to the company.
2. Change their identities from consultants to salespeople.
3. Change the structure of their organization.

Through the medium of the universal solvent, which we described in Chapter 2, employees were given an opportunity to express their opinions on several critical questions regarding the company. These included: What advice do you want to give the CEO on how to improve our market position? What changes are taking place in the market, and what are we doing/not doing to respond to them? What are the strengths of your organization and the company as a whole? What is the current strategy, and how well is it understood? How effective is communication between your department and the rest of the organization? The universal solvent gave employees an opportunity to express their opinions. The fact that the CEO listened also told them that he cared about what they were saying.

As part of the program, employees participated in a simulation game that demonstrated to them how many problems arise because of miscommunication and attributing blame to someone else when things go wrong. Later that day, employees were also led through an analysis of each of the company's major markets, its current requirements, how they were changing, and what the company had to do in order to satisfy the customers. Most of the participants in the program had never thought in these terms before.

Up to this point, the CEO had simply been observing the program. He had not wanted to say anything too early that might have been perceived as an attempt to use the power of his position to force a change on the employees. This might have led to the development of resistance and a powerful antinorm group. Now he arose and presented his vision and his overall corporate strategy, without suggesting how the employees should participate in it. They broke into small groups to discuss how the strategy might be applied in their department. Later they also talked about their own identities as consultants and why a change in this identity might be necessary if they were to function effectively in the marketplace.

While the participants had now intellectually begun to accept the necessity for change, this acceptance also had to occur at an emotional level. So the trainers presented a simulation exercise that enabled the entire group to literally leave behind their old identities and adopt new ones. Then the trainers helped them evaluate the company's products and how to sell them most effectively; whether they felt comfortable selling them; and what support they would need in the field.

While the consultants were now beginning to feel like salespeople, they still hadn't significantly strengthened their commitment to the company. The trainers knew from their information gathering that each of the participants felt exhausted from the amount of travel the job entailed and stressed out from being stretched far too thin trying to serve too many clients. So another simulation exercise was presented to drive home the fact that this situation would be improved only by cooperation and teamwork. These elements could be provided by the firm. It would help the employees form cross-functional teams that supply additional resources and support to make their jobs easier.

As an initial step in this process, several project teams were established to collect the important data that would be necessary before the corporate reorganization could begin. They focused on areas such as training, compensation, communication, and servicing clients more effectively. Assigned to lead each of the teams and report their findings to the CEO was one of the stars among the sales representatives.

If you recall our discussion of the Elites, the Ins, and Outs, these sales representatives had previously felt like Outs, excluded from having any impact on the operation of the company. What the CEO (the Elite) had now done was to form an alliance with the Outs. He appointed some of them to run the project teams instead of giving this assignment to the Ins—the top managers in the department who remained after their boss, the vice president, had been fired. This new alliance was extremely effective in promoting change.

The CEO had demonstrated how to use his power skillfully. Suppose he had simply fired the vice president, appointed a replacement, announced a vision, and set new goals to guide the department. Since he did not have a strong relationship with his employees, he could have engendered enormous resistance that would have resulted in a powerful antinorm group. Many of the consultants might have eventually left, taking their customers with them. Instead, the CEO understood the human nature of his employees. Information gathering had revealed their attitudes as well as how to satisfy their self-interests. These were a major focus of the training program.

The CEO recognized that he had to win over his employees in order to produce alignment with the change process. Thus, throughout the seminar, the participants were not only presented with hard data emphasizing the necessity for change but also given simulation exercises that enabled them to embrace change at an emotional level. (We'll discuss these types of activities in greater detail in later chapters.) Finally, the CEO used his power to direct the formation of new cross-functional teams led by lower-level employees and created an alliance with them. It's somewhat similar to the situation we encountered in discussing the health commissioner who wanted to transform her department.

In the months that lay ahead, the company reorganized itself into a modified matrix structure, with cross-functional teams focused on specific products and markets. The teams were given responsibility for doing their own planning, overseeing their own budgets, even hiring new employees as they needed them. Team members, who were highly enthusiastic about the amount of empowerment they had been given, set about the task of developing new customers, and business substantially improved.

# 6

# Social Process:
# The Engine of Change

During the early 1950s, Mrs. Marian Keech began to receive messages from outer space.[1] According to Mrs. Keech, they came from the planet Clarion, which was inhabited by a superior race of beings who had conquered the evils of war through advanced technology and enlightened ways of thinking. The mission of the Guardians, as these people called themselves, was to bring the benefits of peace to the planet Earth, and they had chosen Mrs. Keech to be their spokesperson.

A Guardian named Sananda told Mrs. Keech that her mission was to "spread the news, tell the story, and be fearless in the doing. The world mind is still in lethargy," he warned. "It does not want to awaken."

Sananda revealed to Mrs. Keech that a great flood would engulf the world before the end of the year, destroying both coastlines of the United States and turning the center of the country into a vast lake. But he also promised that the true believers, like herself, would be saved by the Guardians, whose flying saucers were even then hovering around the Earth and preparing to land.

When a report of the impending cataclysm reached the local newspaper, most people tended to scoff at Mrs. Keech's prophecies. But there were a few who took her words seriously and began to prepare for the flood. One young man sold his earthly possessions to pay off his debts, said good-bye to his parents, and dedicated himself to the movement. Several women quit their jobs to work full time with Mrs. Keech. And her staunchest supporter, a doctor who worked at a local college, was fired for preaching about the coming catastrophe. While she was surrounded

1. This story comes from Leon Festinger, Henry W. Riecken, and Stanley Schacter, *When Prophecy Fails* (New York: Harper, 1964).

by a solid group of devoted followers, others who joined Mrs. Keech were not so committed. They had some doubts about her message. But for the moment they were prepared to watch and wait, preferring salvation if she were correct rather than the soggy alternative.

Although December 21 had been designated as the day of the great flood, Mrs. Keech and her coterie of believers had been promised that they would be picked up beforehand in a flying saucer sent by the Guardians. Mrs. Keech was assured that December 17 would be the date of their rescue. That day, she and her friends searched the heavens for a saucer, but in vain; none ever appeared. There was a general feeling of disappointment among the group. And for a young woman named Manya, a new convert and one of the least committed members, it was enough to convince her to abandon the movement.

Meanwhile, Mrs. Keech had been reassured by Sananda not to despair. A flying saucer would still come for them. That night, Mrs. Keech and her followers were again told to wait for the Guardians' spacecraft, but once more, no one came to rescue them.

As Judgment Day drew closer, reporters and other interested onlookers began to congregate outside Mrs. Keech's house. Although the Prophet and her disciples had already been disappointed twice by the Guardians, this did not prevent them from giving interviews with the press. Indeed, they seemed even more intent on delivering their prophecy as the likelihood of its being fulfilled appeared to grow dimmer. With one day to go before the flood, Mrs. Keech and her group were again ordered to ready themselves at midnight for the flying saucer that would bring them to safety. But as the clock struck twelve and everyone waited expectantly, nothing happened. Visibly shaken, the group seemed to have no explanation. They refused to talk with reporters who wanted to know why the Guardians had never arrived. Could it be that Mrs. Keech and her followers were not to be saved, after all? Had her prophecy failed?

Then Mrs. Keech received another message: ". . . from the mouth of death have ye been delivered," it said. "Not since the beginning of time upon this Earth has there been such a force of Good and light as now floods this room and that which has been loosed within this room now floods the entire Earth." The flood had been canceled, the world saved.

It was too much for some in Mrs. Keech's circle. Those who were not strongly committed drifted away, because they could no longer reconcile their beliefs with reality. They thought the entire incident had been nothing more than a cruel hoax. But not Mrs. Keech and the disciples most closely associated with her. These fervent believers didn't lose faith. They continued to seek publicity for their movement, give interviews, make additional predictions, and even lecture about flying saucers.

## *The Elements of a Social Process*

We began this chapter with the story of Mrs. Keech and the flying saucers because it reveals some significant facets of human nature—which, after all, lies at the foundation of social processes. The relevance of Mrs. Keech's story will become clearer in a few moments, but first we want to talk about social process. In earlier chapters, we introduced it as a vehicle for leveraging human attributes and using power to produce organizational change. Since power and human nature are building blocks for social process, we had to explore these two concepts first. But we've never actually defined what a social process is. So, a bit belatedly, let's define it now.

A social process is a series of events or experiences that utilize our knowledge of individual and group behavior to facilitate change.

There are five key factors that seem to determine the success or failure of a social process:

1. How the goal of the process is presented. For example, does a team leader define the goal clearly, or is it left vague and undetermined?
2. The situation in which the process occurs. For instance, a team's members may support the process, or many of them may be completely unsupportive.
3. The specific relationships and power dynamics that are operating. These were explained in Chapter 5.
4. Human nature—that is, the feelings and needs of the members. Information gathering can enable the leader to understand the self-interests of his subordinates and use the social process as a means of satisfying them. This is a highly useful skill, as we discovered in Chapter 4.
5. The actual activities or events that make up the process and the sequence in which they are presented.

Whether they know it or not, employees use social processes every day, without ever applying this specific term to label what they are doing. Suppose a management team has gathered for its weekly departmental staff meeting.

*The goal:*               The leader of the department explains that she wishes her team to decide whether the organization should develop a new advertising campaign, one that would mark a noticeable change from the past.

| | |
|---|---|
| *The situation:* | The team members have worked together many times in the past. They are open with one another and trust their leader. The department is considered extremely successful by the rest of the organization. |
| *Power dynamics and human feelings:* | The group is cohesive; the members are not defensive about their own turfs, they have few hidden agendas or sacred cows, and power flows relatively smoothly among them. The team draws easily on each member's expertise, and leadership usually devolves on the individual who demonstrates the most expertise in a specific situation. |
| *The activities and their sequence:* | The leader has an agenda that calls for the issue confronting them to be considered in a logical way. First, the problem is defined. Then, facts are presented, and plenty of time is allowed for the team to thoroughly discuss alternatives and a decision. Only if the staff members cannot come to an agreement will the leader step in and make a decision for the entire group. Since everyone trusts her, they will support her action. |

This sounds ideal, and it is. Now, let's start changing some of the elements and the significance of social process will become clearer.

| | |
|---|---|
| *The goal:* | Suppose the leader doesn't clearly define her goal for the meeting. Then the group will be confused about what they are expected to accomplish. If a good relationship exists between the leader and her team, they may be able to convince her to clarify the goal during the meeting. But suppose such a relationship doesn't exist. They are expected to carry out her wishes, but they can't figure out what she wants. The result will be more confusion, and the staff members will feel angry. It is quite likely that no decision will be made, and the social process will fail to accomplish its goal. |
| *The situation:* | Suppose the team doesn't trust its leader. The department is struggling and failing to grow. But the culture does not permit an open, direct challenge to the leader. Covert anger will pervade the |

|                              | meeting, and conversations will seem meaningless and superficial. |
| ---------------------------- | --------------------------------------------------------------- |
| *Power dynamics and human feelings:* | Some staff members have become thoroughly disillusioned with the leader because they believe she is insensitive to their needs and doesn't support their efforts in the department. They have formed a covert antinorm group that will not implement her decisions. Turf battles have erupted among several staff members, undermining efforts to improve the department's performance. |
| *The activities and their sequence:* | Suppose the leader simply presents several alternatives for the advertising campaign, without carefully explaining the problem they are designed to solve. Then she says to her staff members, "What do you think?" Without all the facts, they will feel confused and frustrated. What's more, the leader wants to keep the discussion limited, and so staff members feel that they really don't have an opportunity to express their opinions. At the end of a brief discussion, the leader intervenes and makes the final decision. This leaves most of the staff feeling completely dissatisfied and reinforces their disillusionment with the leader. |

It should be clear from this example how important a role social process plays in what happens inside an organization, and how many factors are necessary to make it work. Centuries ago the Greek mathematician Archimedes, trying to demonstrate the power of the lever to King Hiero II, reportedly told him: "Give me a place to stand and I will move the world." Properly designed, a social process can act like a lever, initiating change in almost any organization. Conversely, a process that is poorly designed can only increase resistance, produce deadlock, and eventually derail an entire change effort. Developing this process is not easy. When an organization confronts the need for major change, it's because the simpler mechanisms and the simpler social processes have not worked. Something more complex is necessary. But no matter how sophisticated the process may be, it still involves the basic elements we just outlined.

Another key point to keep in mind is this: Each social process should be directly connected with the aspects of the organization that need changing. Too often training programs (such as some of the wilderness experiences) seem to transform the individual, but when he or she returns to the organization and tries to apply this new knowledge, the culture proves resistant to change. Indeed, some participants report that the entire experience has been most useful in enabling them to enjoy a more satisfying personal life—which, while not unimportant, hardly achieves the goal of corporate transformation. An effective social process generally offers an opportunity for personal development, which may include improved leadership skills, better coping mechanisms for dealing with stress, or team building, while being directly applicable to the solution of a problem that is critical to the organization.

## Some Basic Aspects of Designing Social Processes

It is not possible in this book to teach the specifics of how to design particular social processes. Rather, it is our intent to teach some general principles, show their enormous utility, and provide examples of how and when to use them. This brings us back to Mrs. Keech and her followers. A key element in designing any social process is understanding human nature, and this story illustrates one of its essential facets: People are prepared to make a strong commitment to a belief system; indeed, some will continue holding on to their beliefs in the face of overwhelming evidence that seems to contradict them. As you recall, Mrs. Keech's followers gave up their jobs and sold their possessions to dedicate themselves to the movement, and a few continued to stick with it even after the flood failed to arrive.

While this may be an extreme example, it illustrates the power of belief systems. Religion is based on a belief system. And one of its strengths is that it enables human beings to explain the unexplainable—to make sense out of a world that might otherwise seem meaningless. Similarly, we form beliefs about how to run an organization. Since no one has any empirical proof of what works best in every situation, we develop belief systems about how an organization should compete in the marketplace, what motivates employees, and how to lead them effectively. We may also hold on to these systems long after they have become invalid and irrelevant. For example, look at how long it took the American automobile companies to change their way of doing business in the face of Japanese competition.

The incredible thing about belief systems is their tremendous power to distort reality. Mrs. Keech and her followers believed that the end of the world was coming. Sounds irrational, doesn't it? But let's look at other beliefs and how they can distort perception and judgment. Adolescents, for example, often believe that their parents really don't understand them, and they may interpret everything a parent does as an effort to control their lives. Prejudice can also arise out of a belief system, which acts as a filter that can distort an individual's view of other people because of their race or their ethnic origins. Prejudice is a very potent, irrational force that is extremely difficult to eliminate, precisely because it is so irrational. Inside an organization, employees may believe that their leaders are interested only in themselves—in maintaining their own perks and privileges at the expense of the rest of the workforce. No matter what the leaders try to do, or how well-intended their initiatives may be for the future of the organization, employees may express skepticism and even demonstrate resistance because they mistrust the leaders.

It's not surprising, then, that when a leader presents employees with a logical argument for the need for change, they may still oppose him or her. The leader is facing a deeply held belief system that can explain away virtually any fact or opinion that is new and different. The real question is how to break into this system to create real learning for the employees.

This brings us again to the story of Mrs. Keech, because it illustrates another important aspect of human nature: the concept of *cognitive dissonance*. This refers to two beliefs that seem contradictory and don't fit together. Human beings are uncomfortable with cognitive dissonance and will try very hard to eliminate it. Those who were less committed to the belief in the prophecy, for example, gave up that belief after the flying saucers didn't arrive or, later, when the deluge didn't materialize. But Mrs. Keech and her faithful disciples reacted differently. They clung to their belief even more strongly, gave interviews, made more predictions, and even tried to attract new followers. As the authors of *When Prophecy Fails* explain, it was as if the believers thought that if they could convince more and more people of the truth of these predictions, they must be true. This was how they tried to eliminate the cognitive dissonance.

The natural human desire to remove cognitive dissonance can be an extremely powerful force for and against change. For years cigarette smokers were presented with data that linked smoking with cancer, heart disease, and emphysema. Some smokers gave up the habit. But many others tried to ignore this information, or they told themselves that the warnings were too extreme, or they chose to believe that these diseases would afflict someone else, not them. This was how they dealt with cognitive dissonance. But eventually, the data became overwhelming, and many smokers simply quit.

By using cognitive dissonance, you can often break into an individual's belief system. If you can prove that something is true, even though it doesn't seem possible within a person's belief system, you have opened up the possibility that real learning will occur. Of course, it is still possible for individuals to deny the truth of the new fact or to come up with other explanations in order to preserve their belief system. However, if the process is correctly structured, the strength of the disconfirmation will be enough to crack the belief system. The time frame is critical, because if new beliefs and activities necessary to support them are not presented quickly, the opportunity for learning may be lost. Change can be terrifying because it involves a leap into the unknown, and anxiety about the unknown can quickly overwhelm people. As a result, they may rapidly go back to their old habits and beliefs.

Suppose you're working with a group of manufacturing managers who need to improve their ability to delegate responsibility. If you show them examples of successful managers, many of them will believe that they already possess the same attributes. If you analyze their style of delegating and point out its shortcomings, they may simply try to disregard what you're telling them. Some trainers even collect data about the managers' style from their subordinates and feed it back to them. These data are often highly critical of the managers' abilities. They set up a cognitive dissonance between the image that the managers have of themselves as leaders and how they are seen by their subordinates. For some managers, this is enough to initiate the change process. In order to eliminate this dissonance, they will make an effort to improve their skills. But many other managers will try to explain away the information. They'll say that their subordinates simply don't understand what delegation really means, or that their subordinates aren't aware of how much delegation is really possible because of the pressures and restrictions of the culture, or that they, the managers, are delegating to the full extent possible given the skills of their subordinates.

Now, suppose you change the social process. You begin by asking the managers to rate the way they expect their subordinates to grade them on their willingness to delegate. Since they haven't seen the data from their subordinates yet, most managers will say that they expect to be rated rather highly. Then you present the data from their subordinates, which show that the subordinates rate their managers poorly as delegators. The issue in front of the managers has now shifted. It is no longer a question of whether they are right or their subordinates are right in terms of how well the managers delegate. It is simply a question of whether the managers accurately predicted how their subordinates would rate them. They can't escape the fact that their predictions were mistaken; there is no other explanation. This creates a powerful cognitive dissonance for most managers, and provides a much stronger platform from which to mount a change process.

What seems like a subtle difference between two ways of presenting information can really have an enormous impact. One way provides a lever to open the belief system and start the learning process. The other, which looks almost identical, often has much less effect. A social process is most effective in changing peoples' beliefs when it is so powerful, so moving for all the participants, that it changes the way they experience things.

Let's take a specific example and see how a carefully designed process can fundamentally change communication. Suppose you wanted to have a discussion about the current situation in your organization and the direction in which you should move in the future. You decide to bring together the top sixty people to develop a working consensus about ten different areas of the company. Let's suppose that every person talks for a minimum of five minutes about each area.

$$60 \text{ people} \times 5 \text{ minutes} \times 10 \text{ topics} = 50 \text{ hours}$$

That's fifty hours for everyone to voice an opinion. And after everyone has spoken, at least another twenty hours would be required for such a large group to reach a consensus.

Of course, what inevitably occurs in this situation is that not everyone speaks. As much as half the group will sit silently and say nothing. Although the other half will raise their hands and volunteer a little information, the proceedings will really be dominated by a few aggressive employees who do most of the talking. Since these people feel that they must compete with one another to hold the floor, they don't try to engage in a dialogue; instead, each simply advocates a position, generally as strongly as possible, in an attempt to influence everyone else. Some of them may even try to guess what you, as their boss, want them to say in hopes of currying favor, while others may intentionally want to provoke you to show their independence. Unfortunately, these highly vocal individuals may not be reflecting the opinions of the rest of the group, who are becoming more and more frustrated and eventually stop listening. As a result, no one is really satisfied—most of the audience does not feel empowered, and you don't obtain accurate feedback.

What if the same task could be accomplished with much better results in only three hours, using a structured process? In the first place, the discussion would be much more likely to occur because the organization would not have to devote so many valuable hours to it. Second, the fact that such a discussion was compressed into such a short time period would also increase its emotional impact. The opportunity for individuals to present candid information in a brief time frame releases enormous energy in any group. The same information dragged out laboriously over a much longer time does not have the same effect. Thus, this process would fundamentally alter the emotional impact of the entire experience. Since human emotions are critical to the change effort, as we have pointed

**Figure 6-1. Arrangement of staff members for the universal solvent.**

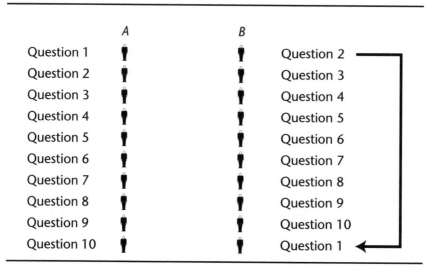

out before, this would be extremely beneficial. How do we do this? The process is the universal solvent, which we described earlier in Chapter 2. Now we'd like to explain it in greater detail so that you can see how a social process works.

Staff members are arranged in lines of 10 (see Figure 6-1). For example, the ten people in line A sit across from their opposite numbers in line B. For sixty people, there would be three pairs of these lines. Each person has a preprinted question about the organization. These questions were developed before the exercise begins through a process of information gathering in which the staff members were asked to talk about the issues and concerns that were on their minds. Examples might be the following: What is the greatest frustration you experience in your job or role? What problems are encountered in bringing new products to market? What strengths does the organization have that help it to be successful in its markets? Each participant keeps the same question throughout the exercise. He asks that question of the person opposite. That person also has a question that she will ask. Each person gets five minutes to respond to the other's question, for a total of ten minutes per round. When each round is over, column B moves counterclockwise—that is, the first person in the line moves to the end, everyone else moves up one place, and new pairs are created. Each participant is instructed that, when asking a question, he or she should simply act as a recorder of the information that is received in response. There should be no attempt to argue with the respondent. At most, all that the person who is asking the question should do is probe for more information. After the interviewing process is over, people with the same question get together and summarize the answers that they received. It's important that they summarize these answers only, not their opinion of them.

As we mentioned in Chapter 2, what results from the universal solvent is an explosion of dialogue and energy. When the lines start to talk, the hum in the room grows almost to a roar, as pent-up opinions are released and flow at a rapid pace from person to person.

Why does this process work so well? First, the powerful individuals in the organization are buried in groups of two, so that they cannot dominate the rest of the group or intimidate anyone else who wants to speak out. Second, most people feel safer and freer to talk in a group of two than in a group of sixty. Therefore, they express themselves more openly. And what they experience is that someone else is finally listening. "At last, I'm getting my message across," each person realizes. "Someone cares about what I have to say." In turn, the listener receives candid information, not a canned response designed to please you, the leader. At last, the truth is coming out. Third, when all the answers to the same question are summarized and presented to the entire group, including yourself, each individual's safety is protected. The information is anonymous, and the individual who is presenting the summary is just reporting what he or she has heard, not his or her own opinion.

The universal solvent demonstrates how a social process, properly structured, can open wide the channels of communication. Let's go back to the key factors we discussed earlier that determine the success of a social process. The goal and the situation have now changed. As a leader, you are no longer soliciting feedback from a group of subordinates in a free-for-all discussion in which only the strongest will really be heard. Instead, each employee is valued as an individual and encouraged to provide information with complete confidentiality to someone whose sole function is to listen, not to agree (or, more likely, disagree, as so often happens in large groups). Thus the power dynamics are different, and each person's human feelings and needs are respected. This gives each participant a greater feeling of individual specialness. Every person is representing his or her own opinion instead of allowing someone else to speak for him or her. The sequence of events is also different. Instead of everyone talking in a freewheeling discussion, individuals first deliver and then receive information one-to-one. Then the answers to each question are gathered together, listed on a flip chart in front of the room, and discussed openly.

As a social process, the universal solvent enables employees to feel empowered. They believe that their message has been heard—that data have been gathered from all of them, not just a few dominant spokespersons. And they are more likely to take action on that input rather than disregarding it as the opinions of a small minority. In addition, the universal solvent provides accurate feedback to you as a leader. Too often, your position stands in the way of receiving honest information from subordinates, who may simply tell you what they think you want to hear in order to preserve their jobs in the organization. This prevents you from really understanding a problem or finding an effective way to fix it. Thus, the universal solvent removes the power of the boss as an obstacle to communication. Furthermore, when the answers are summarized at the end and presented to the boss, the exercise demonstrates dramatically his or her willingness to listen. The entire group sees that the boss is prepared to take in new information and learn from it. This provides a model for them to do the same thing.

Exercises like the universal solvent can be used in social processes that involve not only a single functional area but also groups from different functional areas. As cross-functional teams are formed, members often bring various misconceptions, or stereotypes, about their counterparts from another department. These stereotypes may prevent smooth working relationships among the individuals on the team. Let's suppose that in a computer software company, R&D and sales are expected to work together on a project to open up a new market.

The people from R&D may see themselves as a bunch of "hotshot scientists" and view their opposite numbers in the sales department as lacking a complete understanding of the company's products and the initiative to sell them effectively. The salespeople, on the other hand, may regard R&D as being completely out of touch with the needs of the marketplace, which they understand far better. At the outset, both groups are operating only on what they believe to be true, and these negative stereotypes will more than likely prevent successful cooperation. A social process can help overcome these problems.

By enabling individuals from the different departments to talk together, one to one, the universal solvent can help break down the barriers. They can ask each other questions: "How does your department see itself?" "How do you see us?" "How do you think we see you?" Generally, the answers reveal that while the stereotypes may contain some grains of truth, they hardly represent the entire picture. For example, there are often common elements that unite the two departments. The individuals then discuss methods of overcoming the stereotypes and working together that might be successful in their organization. Following this experience, they go back to their own groups and talk over some of these methods with them. Each group then determines which approaches seem to work best. Finally, the groups share this information with each other and begin to build a team.

As a result of exercises like the universal solvent, a group of employees start to develop a consensus. They not only agree on the problems they confront, but also begin to devise methods for dealing with them. In short, they are building a new belief system. Of course, this takes much more time and far more activities. But once a group of people finally unite around a specific belief system, this represents a potent force for change. Demagogues know the value of this force in carrying out their policies. Adolf Hitler, for example, built a consensus among the German people around his doctrines of hate and used this power to overturn political systems and wage a war of mass destruction. Of course, the same principle can be used for positive change, as well. Martin Luther King, Jr., forged a consensus among a majority of Americans that transformed civil rights laws, overturning centuries of discrimination.

On a smaller scale, organizations that build a consensus among their employees around the necessity for change create enormous energy that can be used to make the transformation process work. The preceding chapter talked about a financial services firm in which a group of employees were being asked to change their roles from consultants to salespeople. This was a difficult transition for most of them, and so the company developed a social process that enabled them to see why their new roles were so critical to the future of their organization. Part of this process included an exercise in which the group built a consensus around the need to assume these new roles.

The entire group (approximately 100 people) was instructed to stand around a table in the center of the room. Then they were asked a question: "Can the consultants use their relationships with clients to sell them mutual funds?" People in the group debated this issue. One might say, "It's unethical for us to be salespeople." Everybody who agreed with that statement was asked to walk to one side of the table; all of those who disagreed remained on the other side. Another person might counter, "If we don't sell, we'll eventually lose all our business." Again, everyone would demonstrate support or opposition by standing on a specific side of the table. As they debated the pros and cons of becoming salespeople, the group would flow from one side of the table to the other. It was impossible for anyone to remain neutral. If you agreed, you remained where you were standing; if you disagreed, you moved. So, even by not moving, you were taking a stand. Gradually, a consensus built around the fact that the consultants had to become salespeople—it was the only way to save their jobs. And everyone could see this consensus building. It was much more powerful than simply asking for a show of hands from all those sitting in the audience who agreed that they must begin selling mutual funds. As the consensus built, it became very difficult for the few who disagreed to stand alone on their side of the table. The large group on the other side seemed too overwhelming. It also provided strength for its members, many of whom still felt anxious about taking on a new role and learning the skills that would be necessary if they were to succeed in it. By physically building a consensus, these employees were also declaring their support for change and creating energy for the change process—energy that proved highly instrumental in making this process work.

By its very nature, a social process like the one we just described lavishes attention on the employees who participate in it. Decades ago, researchers discovered that when management made employees feel special, it increased their willingness to make improvements in how they worked. In studies conducted at Western Electric's Hawthorne plant in Cicero, Illinois, researchers improved lighting conditions and output increased; then they made the lighting conditions worse, and productivity jumped again. These results, known as the *Hawthorne effect,* demonstrated that any attention shown to employees would lead to improvement. The Hawthorne effect is a built-in advantage for social processes, and it can often help them succeed.

The longer you can keep the spotlight on a specific department or work group, the better your chances of success. When employees have sufficient time to vent about problems on the job and to work on solutions, they are more likely to be invested in the results. This principle underlies the development of the universal solvent. At first, participants may feel uncomfortable revealing their attitudes. But the more everyone in the group participates, the more emotionally charged people become. This facilitates the change effort.

## The Engine of Change

What social processes can do, at least on a temporary basis, is alter employees' beliefs. They change their beliefs about themselves, about their colleagues, and about their organizations. By stacking exercises like those just described one after the other, it is possible to create a chain reaction. Morale reaches new heights, motivation soars, and the change process is accelerated. (Of course, without further steps, the results are only temporary—a problem that will be addressed in Chapter 9.)

Successful social processes capitalize on the nature of each situation. For example, if managers are not functioning effectively, you can flood them with information in such a way that it creates a cognitive dissonance that is too powerful for them to ignore. This becomes a source of energy that can fuel the change process. If employees feel frustrated because their organization is not competing effectively in the marketplace, it is possible to create an exercise like the universal solvent that capitalizes on these frustrations and uses them to fuel a discussion that can initiate change. If employees are feeling anxious about assuming new roles and responsibilities in the organization, it is possible to channel that anxiety and use it to help them build a consensus around the need for change.

Thus, the energy to produce change can come from a variety of sources. If an organization is failing, the crisis itself can offer an opportunity for change by capitalizing on employees' fear of losing their jobs. If an organization is thriving, energy can be generated from the excitement over being successful and the desire to do even better. If an entrenched set of middle managers resist change, the energy of their disenfranchised subordinates can be used to overcome this resistance.

Virtually every situation, by its very nature, has the seeds of change present in it. The challenge is to figure out where to apply the leverage. Of course, this involves a clear understanding of human nature (the feelings and self-interests of your employees) and the realities of power. These two elements are critical in developing a successful social process that unleashes enough energy to bring about change.

## *Social Process in Action*

Chapter 4 described the program used by the new manager of a sales department that was suffering from a serious morale problem. Let's look at these training seminars again, but this time as a social process that includes some of the key factors we've described in the previous sections.

▲ Every social process should begin with a clear goal. The message that a boss communicates, usually at the start of a social process, is critically important in setting the tone for everything that follows.

▲ The social process must also take into account the situation that exists in the organization and use that situation to provide energy for change.

▲ The human factor—the attitudes and motivations of employees—should play an important role in designing the process.

▲ The social process must take into account the realities of power: Do the participants form a cohesive group? Is there a strong antinorm group among them? Are there several dominant employees who will try to overshadow everyone else? How can the power of the boss be overcome so that employees feel comfortable in expressing their true feelings?

▲ Finally, a group of activities to achieve the desired goal must be developed and presented in a sequence that will be effective. These activities can utilize such things as the power of cognitive dissonance and consensus building, as well as the elements of the universal solvent.

As you may recall, the manager's vision for the sales department was quite straightforward: He wanted his subordinates to recognize that change was continuous and that they must do more than simply react to it—they must feel empowered to initiate it themselves, for only in this way could they anticipate the needs of the marketplace and serve their customers. But to carry out this vision, the manager realized, his subordinates had to first deal with some important personal issues. So he delivered a powerful message to them. He emphasized that this seminar was primarily designed to help them as individuals by restoring their morale and self-confidence (although he also hoped that doing so would improve the performance of the department).

To accomplish these objectives, a series of experiences were designed that continually moved back and forth between external events and the managers' personal problems. The training session started with the external events affecting the sales department. Next, the managers talked about how the problems in their department were affecting them personally and their families. Following this discussion, the seminar returned to the participants' role as managers by putting them through a series of exercises that evaluated their leadership abilities. The social process was never allowed to stray too far from the problems in the organization, even when the focus was on helping these managers with their own self-improvement.

Earlier, we discussed the role that cognitive dissonance can play in promoting change. By letting the managers predict how their leadership skills would be rated by subordinates, then providing them with the actual results of their subordinates' ratings, the training team created strong cognitive dissonance. The managers' desire to eliminate this dissonance became a catalyst for improving their skills.

After this, the sequence of experiences once more returned to the managers' personal issues with the life charts, on which they graphed their lives in terms of four dimensions: quality of their relationships, sense of achievement, positions of power, and overall life satisfaction. But even this information was tied back to the organization, because the managers used it to better understand not only themselves, but also the motivations of other people (their subordinates, for example) and how to lead them more effectively.

In this social process, the power dimension was important. The manager of the department had used his power to make the entire experience possible. But, following a few opening remarks, he completely disappeared. Without his powerful presence, his subordinates felt much freer to express themselves openly.

It is important to realize that the manager took a considerable risk in designing this training process the way he did. It might have been easier to deal with the productivity issue immediately. But the manager understood the feelings and needs of the participants. They were worn out and disillusioned with the organization, which, they believed, didn't care about them. If the manager had emphasized increased productivity instead of personal growth, he would have undermined all of his efforts to turn around the department. His subordinates probably would have resisted him. Instead of presenting his vision immediately, he selected a more indirect route, one that proved in the end to be more successful. Of course, at the start of the seminar there were no guarantees that the manager could turn around his department following the course he had selected. He had to be willing to take that chance, but prudent risk taking is one of the attributes of successful leadership.

Since this was a social process intended to promote personal growth, the activities were structured so that the participants could not only work individually, but also share as much information as possible in small groups. Here they could discuss new insights into themselves and their roles as managers, feel that they were being heard by their colleagues, and experience a sense of empowerment derived from taking more control of their lives and the operation of their department.

By the end of this program, the managers were infused with renewed energy and self-confidence. They returned to their department and concentrated on improving their leadership styles. But this was only the beginning. Now their new boss needed to have them commit to his vision and develop a specific program to carry it out. Three months later he convened another seminar to accomplish these goals. Since they were different from the previous goals, a different social process was necessary.

Some information that had been gathered showed that the morale of the organization was still very low. Although the managers' outlook had changed as a result of the first seminar, they had not yet been able to turn around their subordinates. The managers talked extensively about this problem and what might be done about it. Then the new boss stood up and presented his vision of where the department should be heading during the months ahead. The importance of this vision and how it could be achieved was the message he wished to communicate in this seminar.

It was absolutely critical that the managers buy into this vision and give it their wholehearted support. If they did not, the change effort would surely fail. As a result of the previous seminar, which had enabled them to achieve satisfying personal growth, the managers were already predisposed to give their new leader some support. But how could he be sure that they were really committed to his vision, not just giving him lip service because of his power in the department?

It's a problem that bedevils every leader. Some seem to settle for the appearance of support from their subordinates. This may look impressive, at least in the short term, but it's not true leadership. And, down the road, their subordinates often undermine the change process. But this manager wanted the real thing, which is usually much harder to achieve. It required altering the power dimension—enabling the leader to obtain feedback from his managers in a way that was not affected by the fact that he had power over them.

Periodically, this book talks about dilemmas. This is one of them. The manager wants honest feedback from his subordinates about their commitment to his vision, but since he has complete power over their jobs, they may be afraid to be honest with him. Real commitment means that the manager's subordinates must have the freedom to decide. Commitment is not something that someone else does to you. You must do it for yourself. Before they become committed, the subordinates want to have their concerns addressed. So far, they have found the new manager to be very supportive. They appreciate the interest he demonstrated in them by developing the first seminar. But they still need to be sure that they can believe in him. They want to be certain that his vision not only will protect them from those forces that have buffeted the department in the past, but has a good chance of being successful in the future. They want him to be honest with them. He, in turn, needs to know whether his answers really satisfy them. But will they be honest? Or will they be too fearful of his power? How will he know if they are just giving him lip service? This is how the dilemma was solved.

The managers broke into small groups to discuss any questions they had regarding the leader's vision. These questions were written anonymously on cards and submitted to the training team. The managers then reassembled as one large group facing the boss, who sat in front of them. The question on the first card was read, and the leader began to answer it.

Needless to say, this can be a highly charged situation for any manager who is trying to persuade his subordinates to buy into a new vision. He is allowing himself to be exposed under the spotlight. If his answers appear disingenuous or if he tries to parry a question by simply presenting the "party line" in hackneyed clichés, he can lose the commitment of his audience before the meeting is even half over, and they will tune out the rest of what he has to say. On the other hand, if he can gain their trust and confidence, they will be far more likely to dedicate themselves to making the change process successful.

The manager of the sales department recognized the risks involved in this type of exercise. And he was willing to take them. But he also needed some assurance that his audience was giving him an honest response. For they could dissemble, too, in order to keep their jobs. So a pile of cards was placed in front of each manager. Some of the cards had green dots on them, and others had red dots. Those managers who believed that the boss was answering a question truthfully, that they could support the answer, and, finally, that they could persuade their subordinates to support it, selected a card with a green dot and placed it face down. If not, they chose a card with a red dot. At the end of each answer, the cards were collected from the managers in the audience, the number of red and green dots totaled, and the tally read aloud.

This process allowed each of the managers to express opinions anonymously. Assuring anonymity changed the power dimension and enabled the leader to receive more honest feedback from his subordinates. If at least 80 percent of the cards did not have a green dot, the leader knew that he did not have the support of his subordinates. Perhaps he only needed to explain himself more clearly. But if another vote still revealed serious doubts among the managers, they would submit more questions about the specific problem area, and continue to vote on the boss's answers.

In the case of the sales department described in this example, very little revoting proved to be necessary. After almost every answer by the boss, the tally was 85 percent, 90 percent, even 95 percent approval. As each result was reported, it created an air of anticipation for the next question. Then the ritual began again: reading the question, listening to the boss's answer, the silent casting of votes by the managers, and the announcement of the results. A consensus was building. Indeed, this entire social process was designed to release the power of consensus. Unlike the seminar three months earlier, which had emphasized small group and individual projects, this one relied on the structure of a large group activity to create momentum for change. Only with this type of activity could the energy of a consensus be created. As each vote revealed a high approval rate, those few managers who had voted against the boss began to be swept up by the consensus. They reasoned that if most of their colleagues could support what he said, they themselves must have misunderstood or overlooked something.

Following this activity, the training team asked all of the managers to stand and make an open declaration of support for their leader's vision. This was a highly emotional moment in which the managers pledged themselves—one for all and all for one. Real change must occur at the emotional level, just as it did for these managers. It involves a personal commitment, which is often expressed in a public ceremony. A ceremony enhances the feeling of group solidarity, that is, the power of consensus.

As these managers stood together and dedicated themselves to their leader's vision, they were holding one another accountable for its success. It would be very difficult now for any of them to back out or make only a half-hearted effort. Instead, they would be expected to make sacrifices to carry out the vision—working longer hours, developing new procedures, persuading their subordinates to participate in the change process, leading that process to success. But, as we saw with Mrs. Keech and her followers, individuals who make the greatest sacrifice and commitment to a new idea are also the ones most likely to give it their greatest support.

For these sales managers, the commitment had already begun. The group experiences in which they participated released enormous energy among them, and with it, they could change the way their organization functioned. The managers began planning these changes during the remainder of the training seminar, and, in the months that followed, carried them out. Within a year, the department's sales had increased 200 percent.

# 7

# Dimensions of Leadership

On September 1, 1939, as Nazi panzer divisions slashed into Poland, George Catlett Marshall was officially sworn in as chief of staff of the United States Army with the rank of temporary four-star general. For the quiet, fifty-eight-year-old Marshall, it had been a long, slow climb to the top of the army establishment—much slower, certainly, than the rise of his flamboyant contemporary Douglas MacArthur, whose gift for self-promotion had helped catapult him to national prominence years earlier. Ironically, Marshall had begun his army service under MacArthur's father, General Arthur MacArthur, who was completing the distasteful duty of suppressing an insurrection in the Philippines after the United States had taken control of the islands during the Spanish-American War. The conflict was marked by brutal savagery on both sides; and, although Marshall was enough of a student of human nature to accept the fact that men were capable of almost any cruelty in the heat of battle, he also recognized that iron discipline was necessary to prevent them from becoming an unruly mob.

After the war, Marshall received a series of routine assignments that seemed to offer few opportunities for an ambitious young officer, yet he made the most of them. At Fort Reno, in Oklahoma Territory, for example, he noticed that the housing for married soldiers had fallen into severe disrepair. One day, when a soldier's wife asked whether he could fix her kitchen, Marshall agreed, but he also issued her a challenge: He would not only repair the kitchen, he would see to it that her entire house was spruced up, but only if she improved the scraggly front yard. When the woman fulfilled her part of the bargain, the house received a new coat of paint in her favorite colors—an arrangement that so impressed the other wives that they accepted it too. Marshall, who believed strongly in notions like partnerships based on self-help and empowerment, would use the same approach on the international stage four decades later, with spectacular results.

Marshall took his first tentative steps onto that stage in June 1917, when he was among the first soldiers to land in Europe as part of the American Expeditionary Force, reinforcing the battle-scarred veterans of Britain and France who had been mired in three years of bloody trench warfare. Acting as liaison between division headquarters and American doughboys in the front lines, Marshall was initiated into a searing ordeal by fire that tested his resolve as a combat officer. For his service on the battlefield, he was eventually assigned to the headquarters staff of General John Pershing, chief of the AEF. Marshall later revealed that Pershing's willingness to subordinate the parochial interests of the United States to the needs of his French and British allies stopped the last great German offensive of World War I and helped secure victory. It was a lesson Marshall would never forget.

After the war, Marshall was posted to China, where he found himself in temporary command of the 15th Infantry during a civil war between rival Chinese factions. Although their positions were threatened by a much larger army loyal to one of the powerful Chinese warlords, Marshall's troops nevertheless stood their ground. Occupying all the road junctions and rail landings, the Americans offered to give the hungry Chinese soldiers food, but only if they put down their arms. While the Chinese might have stormed the American positions, somehow the bluff worked. Marshall had instilled in his men enough pride and self-confidence to face down an opponent that vastly outnumbered them.

In 1927, Marshall brought his leadership abilities to the classroom at the Army Infantry School in Fort Benning, Georgia, where, as assistant commandant in charge of instruction, he earned a reputation for inspiring a generation of soldiers who would later participate in World War II, such as Omar Bradley and Joseph Stillwell. He drove his men hard—although he demanded even more of himself—and those who excelled were marked down in a "little black book" that Marshall would later use to make assignments in wartime.

Long before that time came, however, Marshall was assigned the task of running a series of seventeen youth camps as part of the Civilian Conservation Corps during the Depression. He brought to the task not only enormous energy but a special talent for organization. He established academic programs for boys who needed them, built clubhouses, and even provided instruction in swimming and sailing. But most importantly, Marshall helped the recruits rebuild their self-image—challenging and inspiring these undisciplined boys and shaping them into responsible men.

These were the same skills that Marshall brought to his position as army chief of staff during World War II, where he expanded a fighting force of less than 200,000 to over eight million. He had a talent for select-ing the best military leaders for various theaters of the war—commanders like George Patton, for example—and defending them, even when their behavior sometimes proved controversial, because he knew they were the best men for the job. On his own staff, he tried to pick the most talented people he could find and then delegated responsibility to them. But Mar-shall always made it a point to learn as much about a subject as his sub-ordinates; he had, it seemed, an almost unlimited capacity to absorb information. In his regular briefings before Congress during the war, it was not only this enormous command of the facts that impressed his listeners, but also Marshall's uncompromising honesty, the trust that he inspired, and his reputation for unflinching devotion to principle. President Franklin Roosevelt had learned early in their relationship that his chief of staff would not hesitate to disagree with him. And the president, who was accus-tomed to calling his other associates by their first names, always referred to him as General Marshall. He had that unmistakable presence about him that seems to mark every great leader.

Perhaps his greatest test came after the end of World War II, when, as secretary of state, Marshall introduced the European recovery plan that bears his name. Speaking on June 5, 1947, at Harvard University, he called it a program directed "against hunger, poverty, desperation and chaos." Sensitive to the pride of the European countries that found themselves in severe economic straits following the war, Marshall did not try to impose America's financial power on them, but, instead, called upon their leaders to define their own needs, develop a blueprint for recovery, and then pre-sent it to the United States, which would provide the necessary eco-nomic assistance.

But Marshall was under no illusion that such a program would be immediately accepted by Congress or the American people, simply for hu-manitarian reasons. The Marshall Plan embodied a new vision: a partner-ship between America and Europe, costing far more money and calling for a much greater involvement in postwar affairs than America had ever assumed in the past. Marshall's reputation and his position as secretary of state would take him just so far in convincing skeptics. He also tried to appeal to the very human motives of many Congressmen who had to ap-prove the plan: those who feared that Europe would fall under the yoke of communism unless America undertook a bold recovery program, others who saw themselves as the leaders of this new program if they supported it, and still others whose constituents were working people and business owners who might benefit from the new markets that would open up if Europe regained its economic footing. Nor did Marshall stop with appear-ances before Congress. He also went to the American people, speaking to groups across the country, repeating the same arguments that he had presented in Washington. It is due to the success of the Marshall Plan, perhaps more than any of his other accomplishments, that George Marshall is remembered today. And in recognition of this singular accomplishment, he was honored with the Nobel Peace Prize.

## *What Is Leadership?*

John Gardner, who has written widely on leadership, defines it as "the process of persuasion and example by which an individual induces a group to take action that is in accord with his purposes or the shared purposes of all." Certainly, George Marshall exemplified successful leadership at every stage of his career. Today, the subject of leadership is central to any discussion of the modern organization. Why? Because organizations are much flatter and change in the marketplace is happening much faster. Opportunities come and go quickly, and so they must be seized immediately. There is no time to send decisions up and down a functional silo, and in many cases that silo no longer exists. Employees in every part of an organization must be able to make decisions and persuade other people to follow them. This requires leadership. Some experts have drawn an analogy between the modern organization and the battlefield. They point out that the flattening of corporate hierarchies has made the span of control so much larger that individuals can no longer manage their subordinates, just as a commander on the battlefield cannot manage his troops into battle. Instead, the modern manager, like the army commander, must inspire his troops to storm a hill and defeat the enemy in the face of intense fire. This requires leadership.

No successful large-scale change effort has gone very far without effective leadership throughout an organization. This often requires two things: First, leaders must be trained, because there may not be enough of them, and second, they must be brought on board in support of the change effort. The leaders will move this effort forward if they know how and if they are committed to it. However, they can just as easily destroy a change initiative if they don't know how to support it or simply don't want to go along.

There are long lists of the attributes of a leader and no end of programs designed to teach leadership. Yet the failure rate among corporate leaders is estimated in several surveys to be at least as high as 50 percent. Why can't we do any better? There's an old story about two men who are walking down the street when they see another man on his hands and knees looking for something under a streetlight.

"What are you looking for?" they ask.

"My keys," the other answers.

"Where did you lose them?" they inquire.

"Over there, in the alley," he tells them, pointing his finger.

"Then, why are you looking here?"

"That's where the light is," he replies.

The problem with most leadership programs is that they focus primarily on leadership attributes because these can be measured—that's where we can shine the light. This is not to say that such programs don't play an important role in improving certain skills that are essential for leadership, at least as far as they go. One program, for example, evaluated a manager's leadership style by collecting survey data from several different sources. These included the manager's self-assessment of how well he or she practiced a specific leadership behavior, as well as evaluations from his or her boss, subordinates, and peers. The manager's scores were also displayed as a percentile rating, comparing the performance with that of other executives who had participated in the program. From these data, each manager would know where she or he needed to improve, and specific "development options" were provided by the trainers—exercises that would assist the managers in their professional growth.

This leadership program focused on competencies that fell under four major headings or themes. The first theme was *visioning*, a skill that George Marshall possessed in abundance, along with the ability to generate energy and emotional commitment from others through the effective communication of his vision. This is a critical competency for any leader in an organization because the vision gives employees clarity about where they are going and a belief that what they are involved in is worthwhile. Questions on the survey related to this attribute included: "Do you understand the marketplace and how to meet customer needs?" "Do you provide people with a clear sense of direction by ongoing communication of priorities, strategies, and plans?" "Do you establish clear expectations up front and hold people accountable?" A manager's ratings in these areas, as indicated by peers, bosses, and subordinates, indicated their perception of the manager's competence and whether he or she needed to make improvements.

A second theme was *risk taking* and the manager's ability to deal with opposition. Under this category, one of the important competencies was assertiveness—that is, the leader's ability to defend ideas forcefully and handle resistance effectively. Assertiveness, in turn, requires self-confidence and the ability to initiate action. This section also dealt with the manager's style of conflict management. "Do you identify and address central issues in conflict situations, rather than avoid the issue or engage in delaying tactics?" Managers were told that many people try to avoid conflicts for fear they will tear apart their work groups, while others focus almost exclusively on the issue to be resolved rather than trying to preserve the relationship between the people involved in the conflict. The leadership program emphasized a third approach: negotiation, which deals with both the people and the issues.

The third theme is *credibility.* As you recall, one of Marshall's primary attributes was an unflinching integrity that engendered trust among his associates. In a complex, fast-moving environment, where ambiguity and uncertainty are the order of the day, it is all the more critical that the leader be a person whom people can trust and respect. This often means that the leader needs broad experience and a track record of accomplishment, like the one Marshall possessed. But there are other factors that build trust in a leader, whether that person is a wartime general or a corporate manager. These include a willingness to follow through on promises and commitments, to communicate accurate and reliable information, to project a clear sense of values and to treat people fairly. Training exercises in the leadership program enabled managers with low scores in these areas to improve their competencies.

The fourth theme is called *gaining support.* In order to gain people's support and get them on board with a project, the leader must be able to give them a sense of being empowered and in charge of their part of the action. This involves a willingness to share information with subordinates, delegate authority, and stand up for their right to make decisions. The leader must also have the ability to stimulate innovation and creative problem solving. Such leaders usually have a strongly adaptive style— that is, they are comfortable with ambiguity and change, seeing them as an opportunity and a challenge. Team building is another essential skill for effective leaders. Questions on the survey related to this attribute were: "Do you value bringing together people with different perspectives in order to produce quality solutions?" and "Do you encourage and reward teamwork with individuals from other functions and organizations?" Managers who received significantly lower ratings than their peers on these items often lacked conviction regarding the value of teamwork. They might be relatively effective managers, despite shortcomings in this area, but they typically were not able to create the synergy that is one of the keys to sustaining successful performance.

Finally, managers were evaluated on their ability to get employees to work up to high standards and take responsibility for producing error-free results. This often involves creating a climate in which people believe in themselves and expect to be successful. Managers who score poorly in these areas are given development exercises that will improve their ability to create a high-performance, participative environment.

While this type of program may be useful in improving a manager's leadership skills, it makes a basic assumption: Since there is a high score and a low score on each competency, the higher the rating, the better leader a manager is perceived to be. This assumes that there is one best set of skills for every situation. However, we know that leadership is far more complicated. There is no single style or approach; many different styles seem to be effective. Compare George Marshall with George Patton, for example; both were very successful leaders. And to Marshall's credit, he recognized that various styles of leadership were essential to assure Allied victory in World War II. Clearly, different situations require different approaches to leadership. Woodrow Wilson's idealism proved to be extremely powerful in leading America during wartime. But that same inflexible idealism was of no help in securing approval of the League of Nations, once peace had been achieved. Wilson's tragedy was his inability to adjust his style.

In organizations, no one set of competencies fits every situation. For example, top-level managers who firmly believe in empowerment admit that there have been situations when they simply had to step in and order a change of direction for subordinates who had gone down the wrong track. Unfortunately, these managers said, they had generally waited too long and allowed too much damage to be done before stepping in because they were fearful of stifling employee creativity and initiative. Similarly, visioning may be an important leadership trait, but only if you know when and where to use it. If the new sales manager in the example discussed in Chapters 4 and 6 had announced his vision too early, it might have alienated all the members of his department and increased their resistance to change. In short, a set of competencies is important, but the judgment to know how to utilize them most successfully is even more important.

In addition to defining a specific skill set, experts in the leadership field have also delineated a set of personality traits that many leaders seem to have in common. Some of these traits are inborn, while many others are probably developed through childhood conditioning. Perhaps most important, a leader must possess a strong desire to lead and to experience the sense of power and the feeling of achievement that accompany leadership. Without this "fire in the belly," an individual is not destined to become a leader. The other traits include such things as a high energy level, assertiveness, self-confidence, personal integrity, emotional stability, independence, volubility, conscientiousness, sociability, a tolerance for stress, a willingness to work long hours, and a keen intelligence. However, we also know that employees do not need all of these traits to lead effectively. Indeed, very few people have all of them. Thus, a checklist of leadership traits can take us only part of the way in analyzing why some leaders are successful, others are dismal failures, and many more fall somewhere in between.

Another way to look at leadership is to describe the functions that a leader fulfills. Harvard professor John Kotter, for example, includes functions such as developing a vision and communicating it effectively, creating a strategy to carry out this vision, and building a network of resources to support the strategy and a highly motivated team to execute it. In his book *The General Managers,* Kotter points out that leaders devote considerable time to network building with peers, subordinates, and bosses in order to carry out their agendas. Leaders must also know how to bargain and negotiate with their opposite numbers inside an organization for the limited supply of resources necessary to implement their visions and strategies.

This requires a practical intelligence, which psychologists Richard K. Wagner and Robert J. Sternberg call "street smarts." They define street smarts as on-the-job know-how about the best ways to manage people—subordinates, peers, and superiors—to get projects accomplished. Based on research conducted in cooperation with the Center for Creative Leadership, Wagner and Sternberg point out that the most successful managers are those with the highest level of street smarts.

## Leadership in Organizational Change

The discussion of street smarts brings us closer to some of the issues that, we believe, form the core of effective leadership. These are a practical understanding of human nature, how to use power, and how to develop a social process. While traits and competencies may be important, they are not enough to effect organizational change unless a leader knows how to use these essential three levers. This involves a step-by-step process that requires experience as well as good judgment.

### Begin With Information

In his book *The Leadership Factor,* John Kotter explains that leaders must be adept at synthesizing vast quantities of information. This enables them to spot shifting trends in the marketplace, the changing needs of customers, and new initiatives by the competition. With this information, leaders look for opportunities, then they craft business strategies to take advantage of them. Implementing these strategies, however, may require a significant change within the organization. While the leader may recognize the importance of this, other employees may not share this viewpoint; indeed, they could be highly resistant to change. So leaders need internal information just as much as data about the external environment in order to put their plans into operation.

They must have answers to such questions as: How do employees view the organization—its strengths and weaknesses? How do they see its position in the marketplace? Do they think its position is improving or declining? What changes would they suggest to grow the company's profits and sales? If they were head of their division, what changes would they make in its operations? What do they like about their own jobs and what do they dislike? What is their opinion of management? Do they trust their leaders and feel loyal to them? How do they think management views them?

The answers to these and other questions will bring to the surface attitudes among employees—positive as well as negative—that will enable a leader to plan a change process more effectively. Several years ago, the CEO of a large medical supply company recognized that new technology was changing the market, and that one of his divisions was gradually going to lose its customer base. Unfortunately, the vice president of that division didn't share his boss's judgment, and there seemed to be no way to change his mind. The CEO tried persuasion, showed him market data, even induced one of his colleagues—the chief of another division whom the vice president trusted—to talk to him, but to no avail. Since he was a long-time employee of the company who reputedly commanded enormous loyalty from his subordinates, the CEO hesitated to fire him, for fear of producing enormous turmoil. But he was threatening to derail a critical change effort that was necessary to save his operation.

Eventually, the CEO called in a prominent consulting firm to help with the change process. One of the first steps they took was to gather information from the employees of that division. What they discovered was that many of them recognized that their market niche had been gradually disappearing, even though they weren't sure what to do about it. So they were more receptive to change than their boss. Even more surprising, although the employees generally expressed great confidence in the leadership of the organization, they rated the performance of the vice president as generally unsatisfactory. Contrary to what the CEO believed, they really didn't have a strong loyalty to their boss, which meant that he could be fired and the change process could proceed. And that's exactly what happened.

This information proved to be critically important for the medical supply company's change effort. Unfortunately, it's almost impossible for leaders to collect such data themselves. Most employees are usually inclined to tell the leader only what they think he or she wants to hear. They know where the power lies, how necessary it is to curry favor with the boss, and what might happen to their jobs if they say the "wrong" thing. Indeed, almost anyone perceived as part of top management may receive skewed information about the real state of affairs within an organization. Therefore, basing any significant decisions on these data can lead to significant mistakes.

Outside consulting firms are often much more effective at uncovering employee attitudes because they are a neutral third party, and employees are more likely to communicate openly with them. The information remains confidential, and no direct quotes are attributed to individual employees.

Before embarking on a change effort, it's essential for a leader to collect accurate information and evaluate it. This is the only way to eliminate faulty assumptions about the organization, assumptions that can stand in the way of creative problem solving—like the assumption that the division vice president at the medical supply company couldn't be removed without creating severe turmoil and resentment among his subordinates, or the assumption that most of them might oppose change.

## Understand Yourself

One of the most important types of information for you as a leader to obtain is an accurate perception of yourself. There are many knowledgeable and articulate individuals in leadership positions who have been unable to translate their expertise into visionary leadership. They provide people with ample information, but without a highly consistent and clear direction. Worse, they may send mixed signals. The obstacle is typically not lack of intelligence or conceptual ability, but lack of clarity residing at a deeper personal level. Those who have not sorted out the basic issues of self-identity and life values find it difficult to focus their mental and emotional energies and provide a clear vision for others.

The life charts presented in Chapter 4 are one effective device for enabling managers to learn more about themselves—their values and priorities, their strengths and weaknesses—so that they can become better leaders. Managers also need to obtain feedback from sources they can trust.

For example, a young manager in a family-owned business realized that he was not very successful at motivating his staff. One day he decided to discuss the problem with the director of human resources, a much older man who had acted as his mentor. He explained that his staff had ample opportunity to express their opinions in meetings and that he encouraged their full participation in every decision, so he couldn't understand why they didn't give him more support. The older man suggested that he attend the next staff meeting so that he would have a better understanding of what was occurring. What he discovered was totally at odds with what the young manager had told him. While the manager believed that he was talking only 20 percent of the time, in reality he was dominating the meeting, giving his staff very little opportunity to participate. His perception was completely out of touch with reality. Later, the two men talked about the staff meeting, and the HR director gently pointed out the problem. Further discussions revealed that the young manager, whose father had started the business, was very anxious about his ability to live up to his father's expectations. As a result, he was trying to control all the decisions being made in his department. Once he began to understand himself more clearly, he could begin to improve the situation.

Sometimes, leaders don't accurately perceive the present or can't deal with it successfully because of something that happened in the past. A thirty-something woman left a large consulting business to open her own small firm. Her vision was to create a different type of culture, one with a greater spirit of teamwork and cooperation among the employees, less emphasis on working only for a paycheck, and more interest in finding satisfying projects. As a partner, she took another member of the consulting business—a highly competent individual, but one who had constantly been at odds with top management. While he was delighted to be given the opportunity to start a new firm and his values seemed similar to hers, in fact they were quite different. For him, the most important goal was building a large, financially profitable enterprise. In the early days, while the business was struggling, there was very little friction between them. But as the firm grew more successful, he began to impose his values on the culture. The woman was reluctant to use her power to oppose him. Why? As a child, she had grown up in a family dominated by her mother. Power, in her mind, had a negative connotation. She didn't realize that power could be used positively to carry out her vision and create a firm based on a positive set of values. Her past prevented her from dealing effectively with the present. Gradually, she ceded the leadership of the new business to her partner and eventually left the firm.

Previous career experiences can also get in the way of a manager's ability to deal with current reality. Perhaps in his previous job, a manager saw that self-managed teams did not know how to cooperate with their counterparts in other departments. Once formed, they became new power centers, guarding their turf jealously and resisting outside direction. As a result, he cannot see clearly that conditions are different in the organization he has just joined, that self-managed teams might be successful there, and that many of the mistakes made at his old company can be avoided. Unless he can begin to perceive the current situation more accurately by gathering information and overcoming the attitudes shaped by his past experiences, this manager will probably not become an effective leader in his new job.

## Identify Informal Leaders

The informal leaders in an organization are not necessarily the people with lofty titles. But they are the people that other employees really look to for guidance and direction. Sometimes these leaders represent the largest obstacles to change, because they don't see it as serving their own best interests or the interests of the company. And, since they command such a large following, many other employees are likely to agree with them. Therefore, they have to be identified and courted, just like the formal leaders. Otherwise the change effort will not be successful.

For several years, a software company had grown through acquisitions. However, a stumbling block to the success of this strategy was the fact that none of these acquisitions were absorbed into the organization easily. A year or two would go by, and the acquired company would still be fighting to retain its identity. This created needless conflicts, unnecessary costs, and lost opportunities in the marketplace. But if the CEO tried to exert greater control, many newly acquired employees threatened to leave, taking their skills with them.

The solution to this problem was to identify the informal leaders of the new acquisition during the due diligence phase of negotiations, before the deal was actually consummated. They were identified by groups of interviewers hired by the company, who talked to employees and asked them to name the informal leaders. In addition, the interviewers taught them to draw powergrams, like the ones described in Chapter 5. This provided further evidence of the people with large circles of influence. These leaders were then flown to corporate headquarters, where they went through a series of exercises designed to anonymously elicit their concerns about the acquisition. Then they were paired for a day with employees from the parent company who worked in the same function as they did—sales with sales, new product development with new product development, etc. Together, they shared ideas and perceptions. At the end of the first day, a dinner was held in honor of the informal leaders as a way of welcoming them to the organization. The next day, the CEO and his top management team presented their company values and compared them with those of the acquisition. They often turned out to be quite similar. In addition, the CEO presented his view of how the new acquisition would fit into the organization. The informal leaders were asked to break into small groups and make suggestions regarding the overall plan and how it would affect their organization. Finally, everyone worked together to find areas of integration. Pairs from similar functions (one from the acquisition, one from the parent company) were appointed as co-chairs of committees in charge of meshing the two companies. The results were astounding. The two organizations came together with barely a hitch.

## Develop a Vision, a Mission, and a Set of Ideals

A vision focuses and sustains energy, whether it's the energy of an individual, a group, or an organization. The scope of your vision will depend on your position—whether you're a unit head, a department head, or a CEO. A good vision provides direction, in both general and specific terms. "We want to be the best medical supply company in our area. This year, we will know we're accomplishing this goal if we achieve the following objectives: a. upgrading our R&D facility; b. increasing our sales by 10 percent; c. achieving a return on investment of 15 percent. Next year, we will. . . ."

What makes a good vision statement so difficult to develop is the problem of separating the possible from the desired. For example, what if it doesn't seem possible to be the best medical supply company in the area? Suppose some other firm already occupies that position, and it will be extremely hard, if not impossible, to knock that firm off that perch. Should the leader try anyway? Or should he develop some other vision for the company? This is the dilemma: The leader must not set the organization up for failure by choosing goals that employees believe are impossible; however, sometimes the impossible happens, and it will certainly never occur without a belief that it is actually feasible.

That's why information is so important. You'd be surprised how many leaders establish a vision for the company without first determining if it will excite any enthusiasm or elicit any support from the rank and file. Nor do they undertake any effort to build that support. It's as if the leader sets a goal simply by considering what meets his or her needs, or the needs of the board or the stockholders. Leaders assume that once they announce it, the organization must embrace it.

As we pointed out in Chapter 3, a vision statement must be powerful emotionally or it won't galvanize employees. They must also find it believable—doable—or they won't support it. Finally, vision statements and corporate ideologies should not be too idealistic, too detailed and specific, right from the start of a change process. It's impossible to identify at the outset all of the values and goals that will be important. And if you try, you're certain to shortchange some of those you identified as circumstances change, which will only lead to skepticism among your employees. Ideals are essential because they provide meaning to mundane activities and enable employees to feel that they are part of something that is much larger than they are. But resist the temptation to start with more than one or two principles; let others evolve as the change process goes along.

## Find the Leverage Points

When leaders confront the necessity of beginning a change process, they are often confronting various dilemmas. If the leader does not initiate change, the situation will grow worse and the company may eventually go bankrupt. If the leader does, it may disrupt the organization and create enormous resistance, and this might eventually destroy the entire enterprise. In this section, we'd like to suggest several ways of dealing with these dilemmas. Each involves identifying and utilizing the proper leverage points.

### Particularize

Suppose operations in your organization have recently been consolidated, and you arrive at your office one morning to find yourself in charge of the marketing department with a mandate to make significant changes. You scrutinize its procedures, evaluate its past performance (successes as well as failures), examine its relationship with the other functions that it serves, survey conditions in the marketplace, study what your competition is doing, and finally proceed to develop a strategy for improvement. But before you begin to implement it, you must ask yourself some questions and gather some accurate data about the internal climate of your new department. If you don't, you may make some faulty assumptions that will derail your entire initiative.

For example, how do people in marketing feel about moving their department in the direction that you want to go? Can you assume that everyone shares the same attitude? Or are there different groups of people, with different attitudes? Is there a dominant group, the Ins, and another group that feels excluded from power, the Outs? Do they disagree about the change effort? Can you form an alliance with one group to convince the other? Are there informal leaders in these groups with significant expert power or moral power that can sway the other members? Are there other individuals, separate from either of these groups, who also wield considerable influence? Have any employees started a pilot program that might serve as a vehicle for change? How successful was it? Has it been suppressed by the Ins and, if so, how can it be set free?

An organization of people is rarely uniform. Therefore, it is a mistake to generalize about people's attitudes. Instead, you need to particularize—look at particular individuals and particular groups, find out where support and resistance lie, overcome the resistance, and leverage the support to make your change initiative successful.

### Go Up a Level

The board of trustees of a small college located in a major Eastern city faced a dilemma. The neighborhood around the college was rapidly deteriorating, and if nothing was done about it, enrollments would begin to decline because students would be afraid to attend school there. On the other hand, the cost of rehabilitating the area was so high that it could easily deplete a large part of the college's endowment, leaving it in serious financial jeopardy. The board eventually hired a new president with strong political connections in Washington, a track record of turning around institutions of higher education, and proven skills as a coalition builder in the last city where he had worked. This president succeeded in securing funds from the federal government, persuading the city to float various bond issues, and convincing other institutions in the area near the college to work together with it to revitalize the neighborhood. Thus, the president succeeded in leveraging a very small investment by his institution into a massive campaign for urban renewal.

To deal with the college's dilemma, the president had gone outside his institution and up to a higher level: the city and federal governments, and other organizations in the area. Since he realized that it was in everyone's best interests to revitalize the neighborhood, he leveraged this into massive financial support for his project.

Politicians use a similar approach all the time to gain support for a program when it encounters resistance. A president, for example, will go over the head of Congress and appeal directly to the voters. Of course, he must make sure that the voters are interested in his message, as Woodrow Wilson discovered when he tried to win approval of the League of Nations.

Inside corporations, a manager who faces resistance from subordinates may appeal to his or her superior for assistance. If you find yourself in this position, however, it's important to be sure that you can depend on your superior for help. One CEO wanted to fire his marketing vice president. He didn't count on the fact that the vice president had strong support on the board. When the CEO went to take action, several powerful members of the board opposed him. He lost face, and eventually left the company.

### Go Down a Level

In Chapter 5, we discussed the health commissioner who wanted to transform her department but faced opposition from her direct reports. In order to deal with this problem, she created new cross-functional teams headed by their immediate subordinates and put them in charge of the change effort. The commissioner had bypassed her top-level subordinates and gone down another level, elevating the managers underneath to positions of power. She knew that they recognized the need for change and were itching for an opportunity to lead the effort. And she used this leverage to initiate her reforms. This is a classic case of an Elite making an alliance with the Outs to produce change.

### Broaden the Playing Field

The CEO of a midsized insurance company realized that his organization had to grow larger or be swallowed up by one of its bigger competitors. Seeing a crisis looming on the horizon, he decided to obtain additional financial backing for his company. With this money, he planned to exploit an opportunity in a major urban market, even though it meant taking on several of the heavyweights in his industry.

This CEO had a clear vision of what he hoped to accomplish. Now, could he convince his board and his top management team to embrace it, too? Fortunately, his track record at the company had been superb. While other providers had floundered, this one had been consistently profitable, due in large part to his steady leadership. Thus, the staff and the board trusted his judgment. What's more, he had shaped a culture that placed a high value on its employees, many of whom had worked for the organization since its inception. They knew that the CEO genuinely cared about them. And, although the expansion plans might mean more work and longer hours, they believed he would never make unreasonable demands on them.

When the insurance company embarked on its expansion program, the CEO realized that he had to hire a new layer of top executives to run functional areas such as marketing and finance. The insurance company needed individuals who possessed far broader expertise than anyone inside his organization—expertise that would be essential as the company entered the big leagues. But the CEO also knew that if he hired a new group of vice presidents, resistance might begin to emerge among the firm's long-time managers, who saw themselves filling these top positions. But the CEO had a solution: He was able to assure all of them that the company's expansion plans would more than triple the number of employees over the next four years. Every manager, therefore, would have a chance to grow with the firm, expanding their departments, enlarging their spans of authority, and greatly increasing the size of their incomes.

This CEO had dealt with the dilemma of whether or not to bring in another layer of management by broadening the playing field. He overcame resistance by giving each of his long-time managers more of what they wanted.

By identifying and utilizing the appropriate leverage points, you can make change far more palatable to employees who might ordinarily resist it. A leverage point gives you a place to intervene in the system and build support for what you're trying to accomplish.

## Check Your Intervention Strategy Against Human Nature

It makes no sense to be too idealistic about human nature or to expect that employees will support your new programs simply because you want them to do so. Human beings represent a mosaic of attitudes and prejudices, motivations and associations, lines of power and channels of influence. Without a full appreciation of these complexities and a thorough knowledge of them, change cannot occur because you'll often be operating on the wrong assumptions. It's not enough to simply develop a vision and a business strategy to carry it out. You also need a strategy to bring people on board in support of that vision or all of your efforts may be wasted.

By taking the pulse of your employees, you can discover where they stand and deepen your understanding of their viewpoints.

Suppose the people who work in customer service blame the transportation department for not making deliveries to customers on time. From the leader's vantage point, with its macro view of the situation, you may realize that the problem is far more complex, involving several other departments. But to solve that problem, you must persuade transportation and customer service to cooperate—a task that will be impossible as long as one department keeps blaming the other for mistakes. By knowing the perspective of the customer service employees, you can begin to design a strategy that will help them change their viewpoint. This might include an intergroup experience. Members of each department can then talk about the image they have of themselves, discuss the way they see the other department, and begin working together to solve common problems.

## Use Power Effectively

Power is essential to make change happen. But it must be used skillfully or too much resistance can develop, which will derail the change initiative. Each of the methods we presented for resolving dilemmas involves a skillful use of power. There are other ways to use power, as well.

The president of a large bank had been hired several years earlier as a change agent. His institution, as well as most of its competitors, was far more interested in increasing the size of its assets than in serving its customers. Apparently, the bank had conveniently lost sight of who was keeping it in business. When the new president came on board, there was strong resistance to him from top managers inside the bank, who believed that one of them should have been promoted to his position. Fortunately, the president possessed expertise in a lucrative new financial market that no one else at the bank really understood. This enabled him to begin developing a successful track record that gradually won over many of the doubters on his staff. Then he began changing the focus of the bank to concentrate on a single, overarching goal: serving the customer.

Of course, there was resistance among some of his management team who didn't share the president's vision. A few of them eventually took early retirement or went to work for another organization. Others were slowly won over by their leader's sheer persistence. Using the power of his office, he shaped an environment that was entirely customer-focused—opening many new branches in supermarkets, providing tellers with the latest technology to speed customer service, supporting the loan departments that dealt directly with local businesses and homeowners. He promoted people who shared his vision, instituted training programs that reoriented employees to the needs of their customers, and each month, at management meetings, made a point of recognizing anyone who had made a significant contribution to customer service.

With this power being exerted from above by the bank president, many managers felt intense pressure to conform to his viewpoint. From below, they saw their subordinates embracing his vision, and this exerted even more pressure on them. Creating pressure from above and below is frequently a powerful way for a leader to overcome resistance among the people in the middle. Once they begin functioning in a new environment, they will often be transformed by the experience and sign on to the change process.

The CEO of a toy company used a similar approach to deal with resistance by one of his managers to operating in a team environment. While other departments, such as marketing and customer service, had readily made the transition, the manager of operations clearly had great difficulty involving his subordinates in the decision-making process. In his previous job—a similar position, but with an entirely different type of consumer product—he had worked with the head of each department, one on one, giving them directives, and they, in turn, had had their staffs carry them out. Since the manager had been employed at this company for many years, he knew every facet of the operation intimately and could keep his finger on the pulse of each activity. But he was not familiar with all the intricacies of toy manufacturing. He needed to rely on his employees, who liked the empowerment their opposite numbers in the other departments had received and wanted to be involved in decision making. Unfortunately, the manager seemed unwilling to trust them. Consequently, mistakes were appearing in his area—mistakes that he tried to cover up, until the CEO finally got wind of them. He tried talking to the operations manager, but that had very little impact. While the man was afraid of making mistakes, he seemed even more fearful of allowing one iota of control to slip from his grasp.

So the CEO decided to try a different approach. Each week he put the manager and his direct reports into a team planning meeting that included the CEO and people from the other functional areas. Every time the operations manager would introduce a proposal that was not carefully thought out with his subordinates, the CEO and the other managers would tell him so. And his subordinates would tell him the same thing. In effect, pressure was being applied on him from the top, the sides, and below to force him to accept the reality of the team environment. Gradually, he began to conform—he wanted to keep his job and the high salary he was earning. He also respected the CEO and recognized that he was trying to save his job, instead of summarily firing him. Eventually, his decisions improved, he began to feel like a successful leader, and he felt comfortable operating in a team environment.

The CEO had used his power effectively, defining a new reality for the operations manager and deftly applying pressure to achieve his objectives.

## Create a Social Process

A little data gathering among subordinates can often tell a leader which issues are troubling them, what their priorities are, where the resistance is, and what leverage points can be used to motivate people to change. Then the leader can begin to develop a social process that will move employees from where they are to where she or he wants them to be, a process that will enable them to adopt the leader's perspective, while also providing some input into it themselves.

To accomplish this, the proper sequence of events is essential. Otherwise, employees may not embrace the leader's perspective, resistance may increase, and the leader may try to deal with it by an inappropriate use of power that will only lock up the system and derail the change effort. Instead of applying power directly, the leader can use it to properly structure the social process. As we mentioned in the preceding chapter, such things as cognitive dissonance, the Hawthorne effect, the universal solvent, and the power of consensus building can create tremendous momentum for change among employees, bringing them on board in support of what a leader is trying to accomplish. By structuring the process, the experience, the CEO assures that everyone will come out to-gether at the same place. This may mean that everybody shares the same perspective that the leader holds now, or together they may shape a some-what different perspective. But everyone will be moving forward on the same journey, in the same direction.

## Create Alignment and Identification With the Change Process and Provide Follow-Up and Reinforcement

These are the final steps in the process of leading organizational change. The first—the use of alignment and identification—is so important that the next chapter is entirely devoted to it. Then we will have more to say about the last step, keeping the change effort going.

As we have suggested throughout this chapter, leadership is far more than traits, attributes, or functions; it is a process, one based on broad experience and sound judgment. The mastery of this process distin-guishes great leaders from their mediocre peers.

# Part Three

# Ensuring Continued Success

# 8

# Keeping Change on Course: Identification and Alignment

On August 19, 1991, startled viewers watched as a special bulletin suddenly appeared on television screens throughout Moscow. An announcer explained that President Mikhail Gorbachev had been taken ill, a state of emergency existed, and a new governing committee was assuming power. Of course, Gorbachev wasn't sick at all. He and his wife Raisa were being held under house arrest at their dacha on the Crimean Sea, and all the telephone lines from their comfortable vacation home had been severed. Gorbachev had become the victim of a right-wing coup.

The leaders of the plot, whom the president had appointed to their high positions in the Soviet government, had become convinced that he was leading the country in the wrong direction, a direction that would lead to the destruction of the Communist Party and the USSR by the forces of democratization that Gorbachev had unleashed. Unfortunately for the plotters, the genie was already out of the bottle and these forces were far too strong to be contained again. Thousands of Muscovites, led by Boris Yeltsin, the newly elected head of the Russian Republic, took to the streets to protest the coup. The army refused to attack Yeltsin, who barricaded himself inside the Russian White House with many of his followers, where he told the world that the democratic movement would not be destroyed. By contrast, the plotters had appeared weak and confused when they held their first televised press conference. As their spokesman Gennady Yanayev tried to explain what had happened, one of his confederates would later

129

admit, "I knew we were finished then. I looked at Yanayev's shaking hands and I knew. I was used to Gorbachev—always confident and smooth."[1]

Indeed, the coup was over almost before it had begun. Around the country, protesters turned out by the hundreds of thousands to show their support for democracy and prevent the country from returning to dictatorship. By the third day, the Communist leaders were on their way to the Crimea, where they capitulated to Gorbachev. The president returned to Moscow, but it was an empty triumph. Leadership was already slipping from his grasp into the hands of his rival, Yeltsin, and by the end of the year, Gorbachev would no longer be in power. Indeed, the Soviet Union would be no more.

Unquestionably, this was not the result that Gorbachev had intended when he had become general secretary six years earlier and launched the fateful process that would transform his country. In 1985, the USSR had been facing a grave economic crisis, corruption in the party was rampant, and a general malaise fueled by widespread alcoholism was gripping the Soviet people. Gorbachev tried to deal with these problems by enacting new, more stringent laws against alcohol consumption and removing scores of party functionaries. He also began exhorting the Soviet people to work harder and improve the faltering economy. Relying on a style he had perfected while serving as a regional party leader in Stavropol, Gorbachev engaged workers at factories and agricultural collectives in one-on-one conversations. He urged them to take responsibility for the quality of what they produced—a quality that was notoriously bad, as anyone who purchased a Russian television could attest—and explained that they couldn't expect the government to improve the economy single-handedly; every citizen must take the initiative. Gorbachev repeated his message on television, utilizing the media like no other Soviet leader before him. Reformers, whom he had brought into the party, developed plans to decentralize the economy and promote limited free enterprise, a process known as *perestroika,* or restructuring.

While these programs achieved limited success, the great mass of the Soviet people seemed genuinely mystified about what Gorbachev expected from them. For decades they had been taught to rely on the Communist Party for everything. The party told them what to think and how to act. In return for total obedience, they had received, if not the the lavish lifestyle that people enjoyed in the West, at least the security of guaranteed wages and full employment, no matter what the quality of their work, and controlled prices that enabled them to afford life's basic necessities. Now, it seemed, Comrade Gorbachev wanted to remake the identity of

1. Neil Felsham, *Gorbachev, Yeltsin and the Last Days of the Soviet Empire* (New York: St. Martin's, 1992), 22.

every Soviet citizen. But they lacked the skills to suddenly transform themselves, or the self-confidence that they needed to succeed. What's more, he didn't seem to be offering very much in return; his vaunted economic reforms were making the lives of most people worse, not better.

Gorbachev realized that *perestroika* would not be successful unless Soviet citizens could somehow be induced to question their faith in the Communist system as it currently existed and begin to think for themselves. In an effort he hoped would enable them to disconfirm their past, the general secretary introduced *glasnost,* or openness. *Glasnost* precipitated a cultural revolution that vastly undermined the strength of Communist ideology. Soviet intellectuals were induced to shine the spotlight of truth on the abuses of the Stalinist regime, anti-Communist books and films that had previously been banned were now permitted to be shown to the public, and imprisoned Soviet dissidents were granted amnesty, among them the Nobel Prize–winning physicist Andrei Sakharov.

Gorbachev had hoped to restructure socialism and save the Soviet system by revitalizing it. Instead, he was opening up a Pandora's box that could never be shut again. Sakharov, for example, was elected to the Congress of People's Deputies, which was part of Gorbachev's far-reaching political changes known as *demokratizatsia.* Hoping to add credibility to the party, Gorbachev proposed new electoral laws forcing its members to run against opposition candidates for seats in local governing bodies and in a new national congress. A surprising number of them lost to radicals such as Sakharov, which undermined party strength. And Gorbachev found himself facing a congress that proved far more difficult to control than he had anticipated. Instead of showing gratitude to their leader for his efforts at democratization, dissidents like Sakharov challenged Gorbachev's policies and warned that too much power was concentrated in his hands. Millions of people who watched these proceedings on television realized, if they had not known it before, that their leader no longer commanded the same respect as former Soviet bosses. Simultaneously, party hacks were being driven out of office by discontent at the local level, and the failure of Gorbachev's economic programs was daily being exposed by the press, which had been granted greater freedom under *glasnost.*

As Gorbachev stripped away the old Communist ideology and emasculated the power of the party, he did not succeed in replacing them with anything else. The past was dying, but the future was unknown, and many people found themselves falling victim to a dog-eat-dog environment in which they were expected to look out for themselves. Meanwhile, there were demands for independence by many of the subject peoples within the Soviet empire—Lithuanians, Latvians, Estonians, Georgians, and Azerbaijanis—who hoped to throw off the Communist yoke.

Although Gorbachev tried to hold the country together by a show of military force in the Baltics, it could not hide the fact that the central power in Moscow was actually growing weaker. Massive labor strikes posed a major challenge to his authority and may have persuaded him to eventually sign an agreement with the republics acknowledging their increasing power. It was this agreement that proved the last straw for the conservatives within the party and provoked their attempted coup.

Although Gorbachev survived, he was publicly humiliated by Yeltsin for allowing party leaders, whom he had appointed, to attempt an over-throw of the government. In Russia and the other republics, the party was outlawed and its political apparatus dismantled. By the end of the year, Yeltsin and the Russian government had assumed the powers formerly ex-ercised by the USSR and formed a loose confederation with many of the other republics. On December 25, Gorbachev resigned. The red flag over the Kremlin was taken down, and the Soviet Union disappeared.

While Gorbachev's leadership led to the demise of an extremely for-midable adversary (a result we in the West might applaud), this was cer-tainly not the goal he had hoped to achieve when he launched *perestroika* and *glasnost*. And therein lies an important lesson that may have particu-lar relevance to managing the change process in organizations. Once a leader initiates change, it can easily lead somewhere that he or she doesn't want it to go, as the leader loses the ability to guide it successfully. We're not suggesting that any leader can be fully aware of all the conse-quences of a change process at the outset. But Gorbachev's experience graphically portrays how decisively things can fall off track, at least as far as what he intended.

Another significant lesson in this story is the importance of an ideol-ogy—a glue—to hold things together as the change effort is under way. There was no glue in the Soviet Union once Gorbachev had removed people's faith in Communism, the party, and finally his leadership. A core set of unifying beliefs with which people can strongly identify is needed to keep them closely aligned with the center. Without this, the system began flying apart into disparate political groups and independent repub-lics with their own centers of competing power. Individuals no longer identified with a central core of beliefs, but only with their own interests or those of their ethnic and nationalist groups, which led to increased turmoil.

Is there any similarity between this experience and what is currently happening inside modern organizations? Far more, perhaps, than we may realize. In the past, employees felt a strong attachment to the company for which they worked. Whether it was Ma Bell, IBM, or General Electric, they identified with those values that epitomized their organization. It was an emotional allegiance, almost like the patriotic feelings that are engendered by a flag or national anthem. And in return for their loyalty, employees had the security of lifetime jobs. Unfortunately, these cultures often seemed too inflexible to permit change. And eventually they were totally undermined by the onslaught of restructuring and layoffs that broke the contract between an employer and its employees.

Currently the overwhelming majority of companies are struggling with the problem of how to create a culture that employees can identify with when these same employees can no longer depend on loyalty and security from their companies. Organizations have tried to deal with this issue by empowering workers and telling them that they should concentrate on expanding their own repertoire of skills so that they will be marketable in the event of a layoff. In short, it's a culture that states: Don't identify with us any longer; rely only on yourself. But this seems to create greater fragmentation as well as insecurity.

People are by nature social animals, and they generally need something to believe in that's greater than they are. Perhaps it's their family or their church, their service club or fraternal lodge, their alma mater or their company. This gives them a sense of purpose and adds greater meaning to their lives.

For many organizations, the solution seemed to be the team-based culture. Let's empower work teams, companies decided, and make them the engines of productivity. Unfortunately, many organizations have discovered that while employees feel a loyalty to their teams, the teams themselves are not strongly identified with any central core of beliefs, any overarching vision. As a result, they often work at cross-purposes with one another and with the company. One of the overriding issues for many organizations today is how to revitalize a powerful belief system, one that engenders commitment to the company while being flexible enough to permit change. Without this, as we shall see, the change process can easily get off track and proceed in the wrong direction.

## Trouble With Teams

Several years ago, a financial services firm had decided to reorganize itself to serve customers more effectively. The CEO had developed a new vision and a core set of values that were heavily customer-focused, and he wanted to restructure his organization along these lines. For each of the major markets, the restructuring called for creating a cross-functional product/customer team consisting of sales, finance, and product development people. Reporting to them would be sales teams and product teams for each of the markets. All of these teams were fully empowered to write their own business plans and acquire the resources necessary to carry them out; this might mean drawing on the financial reserves of the company, using the skills of employees on their own teams and teams in other areas, or hiring additional employees, if they were needed.

The company prepared an extensive program designed to train the team leaders to participate in this change effort. It focused on what their responsibilities were to the other members of the team and how to develop a vision and a mission for their team that were consistent with the overarching goals of the organization. The leaders also examined the current problems that prevented greater customer satisfaction, and shaped programs to overcome these problems. Then they returned to their teams to facilitate this process.

The firm's employees were very enthusiastic about this new initiative. For the first time they felt fully involved in running the business. Their ideas were being actively solicited and applied to the continuous improvement of the organization. They were empowered to serve customers in the ways that they thought best, instead of relying on their bosses to make these decisions for them. Finally, each team would be recognized for its contribution to improved profitability and compensated according to its performance.

As the project began, everyone had heady expectations of success. Indeed, employees experienced an enormous sense of exhilaration as their teams gathered to develop customer-focused business plans. As these plans were approved, the teams received the resources they needed and even hired additional employees to implement their programs. Sales showed an initial improvement. The change process seemed to be working.

But problems had already begun to appear. On some of the teams, the participants never succeeded in working together smoothly. They had communication problems, they didn't know how to structure team meetings to get things accomplished, they couldn't reach a consensus or make decisions, and very little of substantive value resulted. Teams in different functional areas were also experiencing serious difficulty cooperating with one another to carry out their business plans. In retrospect, this shouldn't have been surprising. People who had never worked together were suddenly asked to do things differently without ever being taught how (almost like the Russians under Gorbachev). Overnight, they were expected to tear down the barriers that had divided their area from the one next door where their colleagues worked, give up control over the expertise that they possessed, and share it with other employees on the other side of the wall. This meant they had to overcome the natural feeling of "Why should I tell you everything?" and change it to "All of us need to know everything so that we can work together." It required a different mind-set, which was very hard for employees to adopt. And while many claimed that they were trying to be cooperative, they frequently blamed their counterparts in other areas for not meeting them halfway and stonewalling their efforts.

Another significant problem was that teams lost sight of the firm's overarching mission in an effort to achieve their own goals. While employees knew about the company's values, these had not been completely absorbed and, therefore, did not prove strong enough to guide them, especially if they conflicted with the success of the team. As they pursued their own business plans, the teams lost sight of the big picture. Customer service in some areas suffered because teams couldn't cooperate. Each team also spent money lavishly, often hiring a substantial number of additional employees, to execute its programs. Eventually, this so undermined the financial stability of the company that the CEO was forced to intervene and fire most of the new hires. As a result, employees rapidly lost faith in his commitment to empowerment and began to sour on the entire change initiative. What had begun as an effort to make a positive transformation in the company had gone off track, causing serious damage.

## Identification

In a revealing article in *Training* magazine, the writer states, "Teams may be the antidote to bureaucracy, but do we really know the antidotes for wayward teams?" Companies are sadly discovering that teams come with their own set of problems. They often fail to communicate with one another or cooperate effectively; even more significantly, they concentrate on the trees instead of the forest, carrying out their own agendas in an effort to be successful, often to the detriment of the rest of the organization.

A team-based culture emphasizes employee involvement and empowerment. It recognizes employees for their contributions, compensates them for their achievements, and promotes open communication throughout the workplace. These are the elements that are supposed to build commitment to an organization, to take the place of the sense of loyalty between employers and employees that existed before the days of massive restructuring and layoffs.

What we're finding, however, is that these elements are simply not enough. Employees' loyalty may mainly be directed not to their organization but to their team or unit. And many employees do not have even this affiliation, because they've learned to look out only for themselves. To them, empowerment means that they should concentrate on developing their own skills. Often at the company's expense and through its training programs, they become experienced veterans. Then, like valuable free agents in professional sports, those with the best skills sell themselves to the highest bidder, stay there for a time, and move on again.

One reason why inducements like empowerment and compensation aren't sufficient to bind many employees to an organization is this: They operate on too rational a level. By contrast, the strongest corporate cultures reach much deeper; they go to the emotional core of an individual's personality. Employees really feel something when they talk about their organization—call it a sense of pride in belonging to it, a feeling of exhilaration, an inner strength that comes from being part of an entity larger than themselves.

We call this *identification*. The dictionary defines identification as a process by which individuals gain gratification, emotional support, or relief from anxiety by attributing to themselves, consciously or unconsciously, the characteristics of another person or group.

An excellent example is the way fans identify with a professional sports team. They receive no compensation from the team; no one listens to their suggestions or empowers them to make decisions for the players. Yet they identify with their team, whether it has a losing season or wins a World Series or Super Bowl. They attend the games, often traveling long distances, root for their favorite players, participate in team rallies, and cheer the team on to victory. Fans seem to derive enormous emotional gratification from identifying with their team and proudly announcing, "I am a Chicago Bears fan" or "I'm a Yankee fan." If you asked them why they feel this way, they might be hard put to explain the reason because it defies rational explanation.

Identification is a highly potent force that begins in childhood. It's the way all of us learn—by watching our parents and incorporating what they do into our behaviors. Parents function as our role models, and we internalize their actions and repeat them without even thinking about the process. Watch little girls or little boys in a play group: They mimic the gestures and mouth the words of their parents because they identify with them. A similar thing happens when these children begin attending school. In order to deal with the insecurity of being thrust into a new environment, they will instinctively look for older children to follow and then emulate these role models. In adolescence, another upheaval occurs, impelling teenagers to look around for emotional support again. And they automatically turn to peers or media stars, and identify with their behavior.

The process of identification does not end with adolescence, of course. As adults, we continue to identify with the cultural values and beliefs we've absorbed as children. We may also begin to internalize new values that come to us from a social group, a political party, or a charismatic leader. These forces prove to be especially powerful during periods of crisis, when human beings are most in need of a compelling leader and a strong belief system to relieve their anxiety and provide them with a sense of direction.

Perhaps the most vivid example of this phenomenon, at least in the twentieth century, is the rise of Nazism. The German people came to identify with their Führer, Adolf Hitler, who promised to rescue them from the political and economic crisis of the 1930s, tear up the Versailles Treaty, which had humiliated Germany after World War I, and restore the nation to its rightful position of power in world affairs. The Nazis were masters at staging vast public ceremonies, carefully orchestrated to build enthusiasm and support for their movement. Huge crowds of Germans marched in torchlight processions and swore their allegiance to Hitler and the values of National Socialism. The insignia on the Nazi flag—a black swastika on a blood-red field—became the symbol of the new Germany, emblazoned on everything from personal clothing to public buildings. Individualism in Germany ceased as citizens subordinated themselves to the will of the state and in the process redefined themselves, assuming a new identity as Nazis. And in the name of Nazism, they were prepared to sacrifice themselves, even if it meant dying on the battlefield, because they believed fervently in what they were doing. It was a cause much greater than any of them, a cause personified by their Führer, who created an emotional bond with the German people that proved strong enough to carry all of them to the brink of world domination.

Hitler and Nazism demonstrate the power of identification used in the service of an evil agenda. But identification can prove just as powerful when people pursue benevolent goals. In Christian churches, for example, believers identify with the teachings of Christ. Through public ceremonies they are cleansed of past sins, they take on new identities as members of their church, and they affirm their belief in Christ and his values. Christianity is founded on sacrifice—Christ's sacrifice on the cross—and it asks that all true Christians be prepared to sacrifice their own selfish desires to help other people and carry out Christ's principles. For many believers, Christianity provides tremendous emotional support, especially in times of crisis. People who belong to a church feel that they are members of an organization, as well as believers in a system of values, much larger than themselves, and they gather enormous strength from identifying with it. This strength accounts, at least in part, for the vast charitable works that many churches conduct each year, enlisting the dedicated support of their members in service to their communities.

As the previous examples illustrate, identification includes several key elements:

▲ *Internalization of a set of values and beliefs.* There is no objective social reality. All individuals operate in accordance with an internalized set of values and beliefs that influence what they do and how they feel about themselves. These values can come from a family, a social group, a religion, or a corporate culture.

A young engineer at a major chemical firm that had experienced repeated downsizings was regularly working sixty hours a week. This gave her very little time to spend with her two children. The engineer talked of worrying constantly about the responsibilities of her job and being so stressed out that she could not sleep. When asked how long she could keep up this pace before burning out, the engineer explained that the company expected it of her. What's more, she firmly believed that the organization should continue downsizing, even if this meant she would have to take on still more work, because, in her eyes, there continued to be more employees working there than the firm really needed. Clearly, the engineer had internalized the values of her culture—working longer hours, continually doing more with fewer people—even though it might be jeopardizing her own health and her family relationships. As she put it, she was setting a good example for her children, who saw that hard work was the only way to get ahead.

▲ *Personal investment and sacrifice.* This is another element of identification. Perhaps it means working long hours, like the engineer, or investing time and energy to do charity work in the community; or, as we discussed in Chapter 6, people may decide to sacrifice their jobs to join a group that believes in flying saucers, visitors from outer space, and the imminent apocalypse.

▲ *Public renunciation of previous social ties.* The people who joined Mrs. Keech's group were also forced to give up their past social relationships—indeed, most of their friends laughed at them for believing in such "nonsense." But these previous ties seemed far less significant to them than maintaining membership in the new group. As another example, an employee who leaves one organization to work for another often gives up many past relationships. Becoming part of a new organization and fitting in with new coworkers is much more important to him or her than retaining a connection with former coworkers.

▲ *Ceremonies to enhance group cohesion.* The Nazis were masters at these ceremonies. Religious groups utilize them, too. And some of the most successful companies rely on public ceremonies to recognize their corporate heroes and reinforce the cultural values that are essential to their success. These spectacles build solidarity and cohesion among employees through a direct appeal to their emotions that is extremely powerful.

▲ *Public disavowal of previous norms.* When the German people openly swore allegiance to Nazism and their Führer, they renounced their past beliefs in favor of a new set of values. Individuals who join religious cults go through a similar process. A public disavowal of the past combined with a promise, in front of all your peers, to live according to different norms is a highly potent force, because the majority of people are extremely reluctant to go back on their promises and lose face among their friends.

▲ *Reform of self-concept in terms of new organizational values.* If the identification process is strong enough, individuals will redefine themselves in terms of the new set of norms. And conformance to these values will enhance their self-concept. For example, in the past, employees who worked in the strongest corporate cultures thought of themselves, first and foremost, as members of the organization and proudly identified themselves that way to outsiders. "I'm an IBMer."

▲ *Use of symbols to stand for beliefs.* Religions use symbols very effectively to reinforce identification with their values. The symbolism of baptism and communion, as well as the cross itself, continually reminds Christians of their beliefs and renews their faith in them. Organizations traditionally rely on such things as logos and mission statements to symbolize their cultural values. In recent years, however, these have lost much of their potency with employees.

▲ *A cause that is larger than life.* Whether it's a religion, a political group, a charitable organization, or a nation, those who belong to it have this in common: They want something to believe in that seems greater and more important than they are. It's ennobling to dedicate yourself to a meaningful cause, and the most effective leaders are often those who can instill their cause with the greatest appeal. Winston Churchill, Franklin Roosevelt, Martin Luther King, Jr.—these were leaders who knew how to inspire people to make sacrifices. Each of them presented his mission with words that made it seem larger than life and touched a resonant emotional chord in the listeners. This is a key element in the success of the identification process.

## Identification and Alignment in Organizations

Today, identification is critically important to organizations for several reasons. First, it acts as a glue that binds employees together in support of the overarching goals and mission of a business enterprise. This is especially crucial now, because we live in an era of rampant decentralization. We know a manufacturing company, for example, that has decentralized to the point where individual businesses have become semiautonomous fiefdoms. Each is loath to cooperate with the others, taking a "not invented here" attitude when headquarters urges the adoption of another plant's programs for the good of the entire company. Employees feel a strong commitment to their business, but not to the overarching mission of the parent organization. By contrast, individuals who strongly identify with this mission are much more likely to dedicate themselves to its accomplishment.

As we have explained, identification operates on an emotional level. Surveys have shown that employees will not feel bound to a company by the largely rational elements of compensation or empowerment. They are looking for something more—call it a gut-level feeling, a need to believe, an emotional commitment to the values of their organization. Companies that can offer this are much more likely to retain the support of their employees, particularly in times of crisis.

When a crisis occurs, identification can also make it easier for a company to implement a change process. One of the major dilemmas faced by organizations is how to develop a culture that is strong, yet flexible— one that can adapt easily to new currents in the marketplace while retaining the support of its employees. Identification makes this task far more manageable. What's more, if an organization has to make a midcourse correction in the change effort (which frequently proves necessary because not every problem can be foreseen), employees are more apt to accept this decision if they identify with the overriding goals of the company. By contrast, workers who identify strongly only with their team, or with themselves, will be much less willing to understand the need for a change of course.

How do companies achieve a sense of identification among their employees? It varies in different types of organizations (see Figure 8-1).

In a small, *entrepreneurial* organization, for example, employees generally identify with a dynamic leader—the individual who started the business—and dedicate themselves to building the enterprise and making it successful. The organizational structure is usually very loose, and everyone is expected to fill a variety of roles. Frequently, this requires long hours at low pay while the company grows, but the sacrifices seem worthwhile because the employees feel a staunch loyalty to the founder and a strong sense of ownership in the organization.

In the traditional, impersonal *bureaucracy,* by contrast, employees identify not with a leader, but with the rules of the organization: "This is the way we do things around here." At their best, companies like AT&T engendered a spirit of service that became the stuff of American legend. AT&T employees closely identified with this corporate ethic and would routinely venture out in blizzard conditions, if necessary, to ensure that every customer received dependable telephone service. But highly cen-

**Figure 8-1. Identification in different organizational models.**

| Form | Ideology | Design | Identification |
|---|---|---|---|
| Entrepreneurial | Loyalty to leader | Loosely organized | Identification with authority figure |
| Impersonal Bureaucracy | Administrative regularity | Centralized | Identification with rules— "our way of doing things" |
| Participative | Involvement, recognition, appreciation, human relations | Somewhat decentralized | Identification with co-workers |
| Commodity | Financial performance | Decentralized | Identification with self |
| Empowered | Performance and adaptability | Decentralized | Identification with organization/ team |

tralized organizations often prove very inflexible and unresponsive to change. Indeed, they can easily become completely ossified, like those government bureaucracies where employees are strangled by the rules of the system and buried under piles of paperwork.

During the 1960s, many bureaucracies tried to humanize themselves by adopting a *participative* organizational model. This focused on employee involvement and recognition, along with human relations training in T-groups. As a result of this training, a visitor to the State Department, for instance, might walk into someone's office during the middle of the day and find him silently crying. While the T-groups taught employees to express their own feelings and identify with their coworkers, unfortunately not all of this training was tied to carrying out the goals of the organization, which frequently suffered as a result.

Over the past two decades, many businesses have adopted a *commodity* model of organization. Here the emphasis is on financial performance.

These companies decentralize their divisions and view them as commodities, to be bought and sold purely on the basis of the bottom line. And employees are seen as nothing more than pawns in this game, to be hired and fired indiscriminately. Consequently, the employee's identification with the organization disappears. What replaces it is each employee's identification with self—developing his or her own skills and selling them to the highest bidder.

Unfortunately, this is not much of a basis on which to build long-term commitment.

One way companies hoped to deal with this problem was by implementing an *empowered* organizational model. Empowered organizations remain decentralized and emphasize performance as well as adaptability. Their strategy is aimed at educating employees, through such things as training and varied work experiences, to enable them to continually adapt to changes in the marketplace. In an effort to restore a sense of commitment, the organization has empowered employees and employee teams. Open communication assures that top management will listen to the views of subordinates; they are fully involved in the decision-making process, recognized for their accomplishments, and compensated on the basis of their performance. But all of these are largely rational processes, and, as we have explained, it often takes much more to build identification with an organization.

## *Developing Identification*

An earlier section of this chapter described a financial services firm that had adopted an empowered organizational model. Employee teams were supposedly aligned with the CEO's vision and the core values of the company. But as the teams began operating, it soon became apparent that this was not the case at all. The teams were neither closely identified with the mission of their organization, nor able to work with one another to implement any programs. Instead, they went spinning off out of control in pursuit of their own independent agendas. In addition, many of them experienced serious internal problems, as team members found it difficult to work together. Unfortunately, these problems are not peculiar to this firm; many other companies report similar incidents with their empowered work teams.

To deal with this situation, the financial services firm designed an extensive training program aimed at improving the functioning of the teams, and then strengthening their identification with the mission of the organization. Figure 8-2 contains the highlights of the three-day training workshop. A detailed explanation follows.

**Figure 8-2. Highlights of the program for a three-day training workshop.**

I. PROGRAM RATIONALE

Market forces and business realities are driving the company's current emphasis on teams and partnerships. These include teams within functional areas and across functions as well as strategic partnerships with customers. The future of the firm is in partnering.

II. OBJECTIVES

A. Trainers discuss the data gathered from employees before the program. They talked about their reduced expectations of what is possible from a work team; they are overly critical of themselves and other team members because they are not yet "doing it right."

B. Goals of the process for the next three days

▲ Develop a common language about teams
▲ Engage in common experiences in which participants share together as a team
▲ Instill a better understanding of what happens in groups
▲ Develop a stronger commitment to the mission of the organization

III. PROCESS AND CONTENT

A. Two constant characteristics of effective teams

▲ Ability to focus on the task and put resources to work to produce expected outputs
▲ Awareness of the process: how do team members relate to each other and work together—sharing information, making decisions, dividing up the tasks, etc.

B. Exercise to work on task and process

Two teams are paired up together. One team works on a task for seven minutes, while the other team observes them. Afterward, this team gives the first team feedback on how well they were carrying out the task and the process. Then the roles of the two teams are reversed. The exercise continues until each team has spent five periods in each role.

C. Team members and trainers discuss the elements of successful teams.

D. Each team designs an intervention that it thinks will help its counterpart to operate more effectively.

*continues*

## Figure 8-2. Continued.

E. Each team participates in a series of simulation activities in which members experience success as well as failure, learn to trust each other, and work together more effectively. Then they share their feelings about these activities.

F. Self-disclosure activities

▲ Life charts:

Each participant prepares a chart and shares it with the team. Every person is to disclose to other participants things about himself that others would not know and that will help them understand the individual member's feelings regarding relationships, power, and the need for achievement.

Each participant must ask at least one question of the person presenting his life chart. Questions are not designed to challenge what is being presented or provide feedback but only to understand the why and how of the events being described.

▲ Self-disclosure and feedback activity

1. Purpose of feedback; review of guidelines for helpful feedback
2. Activity: Team members pair with each other. One develops 3 questions that she wants answered about the way others perceive her. The questions are given to her partner, who then interviews 4 or 5 people on the team, who write down their responses on cards. Then they deliver the feedback. The process is reversed for the other person in the pair.

G. A discussion of the elements of identification and its importance to the organization

H. Teams working with each other in a larger system

▲ Simulation activities requiring teams to cooperate to be successful. But these prove to be very difficult, resulting in competition and conflict.

▲ Impact of conflict on internal workings of the organization and the relationships with customers

I. A discussion of the team, the organization, and its overarching mission and values

▲ Definition of values

▲ Teams are asked to rate how well the company had done in making each of its values an operating principle that shapes management and individual employee actions.

*continues*

## Figure 8-2. Continued.

J. Team activities
- ▲ Renouncing past norms
- ▲ Making sacrifices
- ▲ Reforming self-concepts
- ▲ Creating symbols
- ▲ Participating in public ceremonies

The workshop began with a discussion of the program rationale: the current business drivers that had led the company to develop cross-functional teams and create partnerships with customers. Then followed a discussion of the results of the data gathered from employees, indicating their disillusionment with the way the teams were functioning. After a discussion of the goals for the workshop, the two characteristics of effective teams were introduced: a focus on the task and a focus on the process of doing it.

A training workshop is, by its very nature, a social process. Its success relies on a clear understanding of human nature and group dynamics to achieve a desired set of goals. To start the process and create momentum, participants usually need to take part in an unfreezing exercise, such as the universal solvent. In this case, the exercise was different—it enabled teams to experience the way they went about working on a task. As each team tried to solve a problem, the members became so concerned with the task of developing an effective solution that they totally forgot about the process by which they went about it—how well they related to one another, shared information, listened to one another's viewpoints, reached a consensus, etc. While a team was engaged in this experience, another team acted as observers and provided feedback at the end of seven minutes. Then the roles were reversed, and the observers worked on a task. After watching the first team, the observers were convinced that they could do a better job. But they didn't, because they also lacked the skills necessary to work together as a team. For example, leadership struggles broke out and conflicts occurred between team members over how to divide up tasks. The exercise continued through five rounds, without the teams making any real improvements. This activity created a strong cognitive dissonance among the participants, which acted as a powerful motivation for them to improve their skills.

Next came a presentation of some information about the essential elements of successful teams—establishing norms for group interaction, setting goals, etc. Pairs of participants, each from a different team, got together and evaluated how well their teams had done on a particular element, then made presentations to the entire group. In this way, participants began to learn about the basic architecture of successful teams. They were also becoming better observers of team behavior, and more reflective about their own participation on a team.

The social process now had some emotional energy as a result of this group activity, and each participant was engaged in self-reflection and individual learning. These are essential ingredients in any change effort.

Next, each team was asked to design an intervention strategy that, the members believed, would enable the other team to operate more effectively. Unfortunately, most of these strategies didn't work. Afterward, all the participants talked about why each strategy proved to be ineffective and how it could have been more successful. Participants now realized that although they may have known more about the essential elements of successful teams, they still had a lot to learn about implementing them. This provided even more energy and stronger motivation to work harder among all the participants. At the same time, they were also learning to work together, exchanging ideas, sharing their frustrations, figuring out approaches to make their teams operate better, and developing trust in one another.

Now each team participated in a series of simulation activities designed to strengthen the members' ability to work together. After each activity, they talked about the experience and how well they performed in it. This built solidarity in the team. Next each team member reflected on his or her own behaviors by preparing a life chart that graphed all the events of his or her life in terms of relationships, the need for achievement, the desire for power, and overall life satisfaction. (Life charts were described in detail in Chapter 4.) Then each person solicited feedback on these behaviors from other members of the team. This enabled all participants to learn more about themselves and to become comfortable with feedback from other people, and increased their involvement in the team. An additional feedback activity reinforced those feelings.

Then the elements of identification and the importance of identifying with the overarching mission of the organization were discussed. The teams were then asked to engage in simulation activities requiring several of them to work together to achieve a goal. This created an enormous conflict. Up to this point, the entire training program had been focused on the individual team, building a sense of solidarity. Now each team was expected to look beyond its own needs to those of other teams. Of course, this was exactly the problem that had arisen inside the company as teams refused to work together to carry out the mission. Thus, the simulation exercise enabled employees to experience the results of their actions and see how destructive they could be. This opened up each participant to the critical importance of not only building cohesion within a team but also finding a way for cohesive teams to work with one another. It was also the only way that the good feelings the participants had experienced when their own teams functioned smoothly could be transferred to the entire organization, where teams had to work together.

As in every effective social process, the sequence of events in this training program was a key to its impact. First, participants had to experience the frustration of operating in dysfunctional teams, in order to have the necessary motivation to work on team building. This team building produced positive feelings and a sense of accomplishment. Then they had to experience the conflict that occurred when strong teams tried to cooperate. This provided energy and motivation to move on to the next step: regaining those positive feelings by learning to work together. This meant identifying with the overarching mission of the organization so that all the teams would be pulling in the same direction, all for one and one for all. At each stage, change had to occur at an emotional level. It was not enough to explain concepts to the participants intellectually. They had to *feel* these things to make a real change.

Now the training program focused on the identification process. As a first step, participants talked about the firm's overarching mission and listed its core values, which included teamwork and satisfying internal and external customers. Then they were asked to rate themselves on how well they were actually living by these values in performing their jobs. The scores were not very high. Next, each team was assigned one of the values and instructed to develop a skit showing what happened when employees failed to implement the value effectively. Some of the skits were very funny; others were far more serious. By participating in this exercise, employees could begin to experience the way their current operating norms were adversely affecting the firm.

Each participant was then expected to prepare a little speech and deliver it to the rest of the group. In the speeches, employees would publicly renounce the past norms. Perhaps an employee who had previously put her own desire for achievement or her team's need for recognition ahead of the rest of the organization would have to change her behavior. This involved a personal sacrifice. It also meant changing her own sense of self, redefining who she was in terms of the core values of the organization.

The employees then participated in a public ceremony. Each of them proclaimed what he or she would do individually to embody the values of the organization and implement them in their jobs. Previously, the employees had been asked to prepare posters and invent symbols that represented what they intended to do. Holding these symbols, every participant pledged in front of his or her coworkers to carry out the firm's values. This was the defining moment of the group activity. Each employee had made a public commitment and would now feel very reluctant to go back on his or her word. It was a highly emotional experience for everyone, which is the very essence of the identification process. Then employees returned to their work areas and tried to live by what they had proclaimed. At regular intervals, they were expected to gather together again, review their progress, and renew their pledges at another public ceremony.

From this brief description, you can see that this program contained the essential elements of identification that were described in the chapter. Like strong corporate cultures, identification operates on the emotional and symbolic level, giving it enormous potency in aligning employees behind the mission of an organization. With identification, the change process will often proceed more smoothly and remain on course.

# 9

# Making Change Work

James Madison has, quite justifiably, been called the Father of the United States Constitution. Ironically, during those hot, muggy days in Philadelphia, as delegates from each state wrangled over the future of our young nation, it was Madison himself who was partly responsible for nearly aborting the birth of America's new government.

The balding, bookish Virginian was a gifted leader with a vision. More than many of his contemporaries, he saw clearly that his nation's governing framework was in desperate need of radical change. Under the Articles of Confederation, a weak central government was dominated by thirteen fractious states, jealously guarding their authority and bickering continuously over issues such as trading rights, the power to tax, and the control of western lands. Indeed, their conflicts had escalated to such a degree that they threatened to tear apart the fabric of the nation.

From his home at Montpelier in the Virginia mountains, Madison designed a new structure that would replace the Articles of Confederation. It called for a strong central government that could override any state laws that would violate the Constitution. This government would have a balance of power between an executive, a judiciary, and a new legislature that would be elected by the people, in contrast to the existing Congress, whose delegates were selected by the state legislatures.

Madison believed firmly that a national government could count on the support of the people only if it was based directly on their consent. It wasn't that he was prepared to put total faith in the average American citizen. He understood the vagaries of human nature too well from his experience in politics, and he knew that the small groups of men who ran the state capitals—men elected by American voters—could easily fall prey to influence and corruption. However, Madison believed that politics on a broader scale—a government that operated nationally—would restrain the darker side of human nature by making it much more difficult for cabals of selfish men to dominate political affairs. But these cabals could be controlled only if Congress were selected by the people, not the politicians who ran the state legislatures.

Fortunately, Madison's call for a new government had the support of some of America's most prominent leaders, men like George Washington (his fellow Virginian), Alexander Hamilton of New York, and James Wilson of Pennsylvania, all delegates to the Constitutional Convention.

Madison had ensured the support of the three large states represented by these men, as well as states like the Carolinas and Georgia that expected to grow larger, by proposing that the new Congress be based on representation proportional to population instead of equal representation for every state, as had existed under the Articles. That, Madison knew, would give him majority support for his proposals in the Constitutional Convention. Ironically, it almost doomed the new Constitution.

While Madison was a keen student of power and human nature when analyzing the state legislatures and the individual American voters, he had a blind spot when it came to his fellow delegates at the convention. A large minority of them, representing the smaller states, were afraid that their interests would be undermined by a national government in which the bigger states held so much power. But Madison and his associates refused to give in. Knowing that they held a majority, they tried to push their plan down the throats of the other delegates until, as one of them put it, the convention was "scarce held together by the strength of a hair." Eventually, the men who were gathered together at the Pennsylvania State House found themselves in a complete deadlock: Even if the large states were to prevail, the small states would not go along with the new Constitution, and it would collapse immediately. Madison had overplayed his hand, and his use of coercive power had created so much resistance that it threatened to derail the entire convention.

In the end, this disaster was averted because some of the delegates recognized the necessity for conciliation. Earlier, Roger Sherman of Connecticut had proposed a compromise that would have preserved proportional representation in one house of Congress while giving each state equal votes in the other. Madison and his allies had refused to consider this proposal; they said it was not consistent with a truly republican form of government, and they were also convinced that they had enough power to make their plan prevail. Now, with the support of men like Benjamin Franklin, this compromise was placed on the floor once again.

"When a broad table is to be made," Franklin said, "and the edges of the planks do not fit, the artist takes a little from both, and makes a good joint." Franklin, who was a better student of power and human nature than Madison, also proposed that the lower house have the authority to originate money bills, thus giving the bigger states some additional influence in the new government. It was a shrewd leverage point that won added support.

Madison and many of his colleagues were still not satisfied and adamantly opposed the compromise. But it was enough for a majority of the delegates. With their powers safeguarded, the small states now championed a stronger central government. The logjam had been broken. A "miracle at Philadelphia" had, indeed, occurred.

## *Reviewing the Elements of Change*

To close this book, we have returned to the Constitutional Convention, for it reminds us how difficult the change process is to execute—even with a leader as brilliant as James Madison, a vision as powerful as the Constitution, and a crisis as severe as the one that gripped America in 1787. As Madison discovered, it also takes a skillful use of the four key levers.

For most organizations, a crisis is the catalyst for change. Perhaps disaster is already knocking at the gates, threatening to engulf a company unless a change in direction can be rapidly executed. Or perhaps a farsighted leader may perceive a serious problem that is already beginning to roll down the tracks, jeopardizing the fortunes of the organization.

In either case, the leader generally calls together the members of the executive management team to assess the situation and develop a strategy to deal with it. This group would probably discuss the company's current performance, evaluate the threats posed by the competition, examine the opportunities in the marketplace, and determine whether the organization has all the necessary strengths, or characteristics, to exploit them. In Chapter 1, we described twelve characteristics, or hallmarks, of organizations that will achieve success in the twenty-first century. These are:

1. *Vision-directed.* Having a key set of principles that influence the company's operation and give employees a strong sense of pride in their organization.
2. *Cross-functional.* Having a culture in which the old functional silos have disappeared and integrated teams of employees from various areas work together to carry out activities such as developing new products and servicing customers.
3. *Flatter and empowered.* Having flattened hierarchies, with individuals at every level of an organization empowered to make decisions.

4. *Networked.* Instead of carrying out every function, partnering with other firms to handle certain activities.
5. *Information-technology–based.* Highly dependent on computer technology and communications systems for internal operations and to maintain relationships with customers and suppliers.
6. *Stakeholder-focused.* Responding not only to the needs of shareholders and employees but to the demands of the larger community.
7. *Flexible/adaptive.* Having a culture that constantly adapts to change, incorporating new ideas into the fabric of its operations and providing employees with abundant opportunities to develop new skills.
8. *Global.* Recognizing the advantages of globalization, from buying services and materials in low-cost areas abroad to developing new overseas markets.
9. *Customer-driven:* Having a complete understanding of the customer's business so that not only can current demands be met but future needs anticipated.
10. *Total quality–focused.* Having a culture in which doing things right the first time is a way of life.
11. *Time-based.* Developing new products quickly and bringing them to the marketplace ahead of the competition.
12. *Innovative.* Having an entrepreneurial spirit that enables the company to identify and take advantage of market opportunities.

These twelve hallmarks provide a set of criteria that managers can use to benchmark their own organization and determine whether it has the characteristics needed to succeed in a turbulent environment. Some of them probably exist already, and others may not be of immediate importance. An organization must begin to prioritize the hallmarks, determine which ones are most critical to acquire, and incorporate them into a change strategy.

Let's graph Company A in terms of the twelve hallmarks—where it is and where it needs to be strategically. This will enable its managers to determine the most important areas in which to concentrate their change efforts (Figure 9-1).

Suppose Company A is in the information business. It is a small company, founded by two college roommates who had invented some new products that gave them a small but highly profitable niche in the marketplace. These highly attractive products enabled the company to perform effectively throughout the entrepreneurial stage. As the company hit the professional management stage, however, problems began to develop. The original products had fueled such phenomenal growth that

# Figure 9-1. Graph of Company A in terms of the twelve hallmarks.

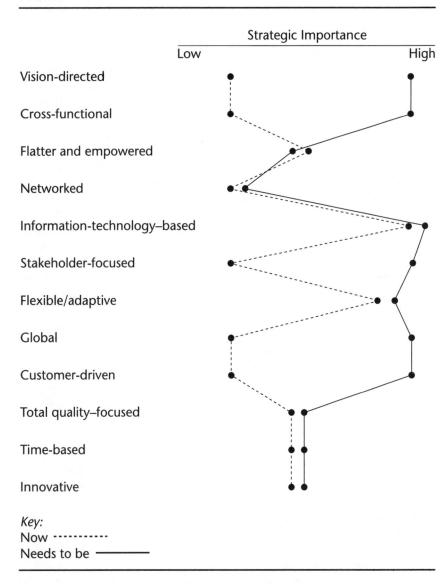

the founders had never established a long-term vision of where they wanted to go when the strength of their initial product line began to diminish. Thus, the company was not very vision-directed, but now it needed to be.

In the early days, the managers had shared roles and worn many hats: manufacturing, sales, marketing, customer service. As the company had grown larger and more people were hired, these functions became separated. Nevertheless, no mechanisms were put in place to promote cooperation and teamwork among the various functional areas. This was creating huge problems, as the salespeople found themselves promising products that manufacturing couldn't produce, and customer service was guaranteeing deliveries that were arriving weeks late or not at all.

Turf battles had broken out among the heads of various departments, which only exacerbated a rapidly deteriorating situation.

Nevertheless, many employees seemed to enjoy working in the organization because it had always placed a fairly high value on empowerment. The founders had a tradition of supporting and rewarding the creative efforts of employees. Strategic alliances with other companies, however, had never been very important to the firm. Nor was this likely to change much in the immediate future because of the niche the firm occupied in the marketplace. On the other hand, the organization was very highly information-technology–driven. Because of the nature of the business, this was an essential prerequisite for success, and it was not an area where much additional effort seemed to be necessary.

However, the firm had totally ignored some of its stakeholders. The government was becoming a major consumer of some of the company's services, and it had no government relations department. The community in which one of the firm's plants was located had begun to complain about the environmental impact of its operations, and so far the firm had completely ignored these complaints. By contrast, the firm had always placed a high premium on lifelong learning, a critical asset in a field that was changing so rapidly. Employees were encouraged to take training courses at nearby colleges, and their tuition was paid by the company; internal training was also made regularly available to employees who wanted to improve their skills.

Although opportunities had arisen in the international sphere, the company seemed totally ignorant of them. From the beginning, its marketing efforts had been focused on domestic customers, and this remained true. Customer satisfaction presented another problem. The firm's products had always been so successful that it had failed to ask what other needs customers might have and how they could be filled. The company did not know about any of the related fields in which its customers did business and how to become involved with them. Recently, the firm had lost two large accounts to a competitor with a less sophisticated product but one that was better integrated into the customers' key businesses.

Total quality had always played a relatively important role in the company's culture. It was not the most critical value, because products became obsolete and had to be replaced by a new generation of technology fairly regularly, and so long-term reliability did not provide an essential competitive advantage. The company had to bring new products to market rapidly (time-based) because of the very nature of the information industry. Fortunately, an exceptionally talented R&D department, led by one of the founders, had enabled the firm to stay ahead of the competition, at least up to now. The firm also had a history of being highly innovative and entrepreneurial.

As Company A looked at this analysis, it could easily see that its most important priorities were developing a vision for the company and becoming more cross-functional and integrated. It also needed to expand into international markets and to focus more effectively on satisfying the expectations of its customers, as well as recognize the interests of its stakeholders. These were the five areas in which the firm needed to concentrate its change efforts.

## Incorporating Several Hallmarks

How does an organization work on several areas simultaneously? Figure 9-2 presents a training program for another company that had to work on some key areas in order to improve its competitive position in the marketplace. These areas included developing a vision, becoming more customer-driven, improving its quality focus, and creating a team-based culture. The program began with a facilitation session for group leaders who would conduct the task modules for company employees. In these sessions, the participants discussed their roles in leading the specific modules and carefully went over all the activities that were included in each of them. Next, there were philosophy seminars for leaders and other employees, focused on areas such as the vision and mission statement of the company; the need for a team-based, highly integrated, cross-functional culture; and the importance of total quality in every operation.

The initial philosophy seminars were followed by the first task module, client satisfaction. In each task module, a group leader was expected to fulfill a variety of roles, which would vary with the outcome the leader was trying to achieve and the needs of the group. At times, the group leader would be expected to directly lead activities, provide information and instructions, and respond to questions and concerns. At other times,

**Figure 9-2. Outline of training program.**

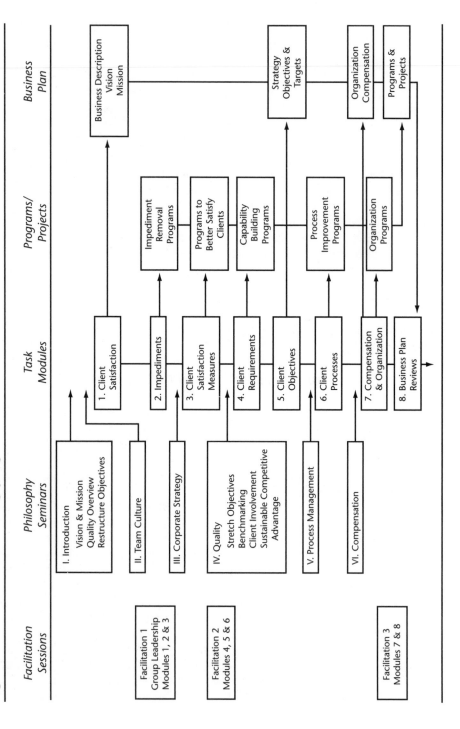

he or she would be expected to take a back seat and foster group interaction through activities designed to enable participants to recognize the need for changing the way they carried out their responsibilities.

For example, in task module 1, client satisfaction, participants were asked to form breakout groups and draw a picture of their business, list their internal and external clients, and state what they do for each client group. Then they were asked to reconvene and report on their results while the leader made separate lists of internal and external clients. Following this activity, participants were asked to make charts for each set of clients, including the following: What are their needs? What makes them satisfied? What makes them dissatisfied? The leader then summarized this information and prioritized the list of satisfiers and dissatisfiers. Finally, the leader assigned a vision task force to distill the group's input regarding the unit's role, clients, client needs, etc., into a "straw" vision statement for its business. Eventually the groups would develop business plans to carry out their vision and to fulfill the client objectives that they identified in later task modules.

Programs and projects were also developed to remove the impediments to client satisfaction, identified in the second task module, and satisfy clients more effectively. Later task modules focused on internal process improvements that would enable the company to increase customer satisfaction and on new compensation systems to reward team accomplishments as the organization made the transition to a team-based culture.

Thousands of employees participated in this training program, which was highly effective at imparting data, assigning specific tasks, and providing follow-up. But, as we've explained throughout this book, real change requires much more than simply providing information, teaching a new skill set, and monitoring the efforts of employees as they try to implement everything that they've learned. Change is a battle for the heart as well as the mind of each individual. This means using the four levers: dealing with human feelings (a natural resistance to change, an anxiety about doing things differently, etc.), ensuring that the people in power are fully aligned with the change effort, creating a social process that persuades employees to embrace change at the gut level, and effectively using leadership skills (information gathering, identifying informal leaders, operating the levers of power and human nature successfully, etc.). It also means finally ensuring that employees identify with the overarching mission of the organization.

Unfortunately, the training program never dealt with these areas. First, the facilitation sessions did not include some of the key informal leaders in the organization. Second, no time was spent in trying to deal with their feelings about the change initiative of the facilitators who were selected to lead the training program. These facilitators had been through other change processes that had not been very successful, and some of them were privately reluctant to stake their reputations on leading another one. They were afraid that some of their colleagues might not support it, leaving them high and dry. In addition, they lacked the skills to operate in this new team-based, customer-centered environment. They were like explorers who had just discovered a new land and didn't understand the culture, couldn't speak the language, and certainly felt uncomfortable leading others. They needed extensive help. But little or no information about their attitudes, feelings, and skills had been gathered, nor were the issues that concerned them ever addressed. What's more, no social process that would have enabled them to internalize the values of the new culture and develop a strong identification with it was ever initiated.

In addition, the facilitators were not taught how to use the four levers to ensure support for the change effort among the participants in their groups. The task modules were very effective at imparting information, but they never dealt with the attitudes and feelings of the participants. Before the change effort began, the company had operated with a "star" culture, in which individual initiative had been heavily rewarded. Suddenly, employees and their leaders were being asked to operate in teams. Unfortunately, they had neither the skills to do so nor an emotional commitment to a team-based culture. And the company never initiated a social process to ensure that the hearts and minds of the employees were fully committed to the new cultural values.

Although the change effort omitted a crucial layer of work, one involving the four levers, some of the teams nonetheless managed to operate successfully, achieving remarkable results. Many others, however, never coalesced as teams because they didn't possess the skills necessary to work together and carry out an achievable set of goals.

Finally, the facilitators had not been fully indoctrinated in the overarching mission of the organization, and so they were not fully identified with it. As a result, the facilitators ran modules for their teams, who, in turn, developed programs and business plans that carried out the mission of their units, but these were not fully tied to the vision and mission statement of the entire organization. The teams went off in their own directions, pursuing their own goals, without considering whether they were fulfilling the overriding goals of the firm. There was no cohesion, no alignment with the central vision.

What's more, the vision statement itself proved to be much too specific and too idealistic. It talked about satisfying the needs of the customers, involving all employees in running the business, trusting their decisions, building a team-based culture, rewarding innovation, and emphasizing total quality in every product and service. As the change effort began to falter, top management was forced to step in and redirect the efforts of the self-directed work teams. Immediately, the value of employee empowerment seemed to be neglected, and employees immediately felt as if they had been betrayed. The company had cracked their belief system.

A primary reason why top management had to step into the process was that the teams were never taught the proper business procedures to use to carry out their tasks successfully. Take the task modules involving client satisfaction, for example. The employees thought they knew what their external customers wanted, based on long personal relationships with some of them and frequent conversations. But this information was not enough. The employees needed to become more deeply involved with their clients' business, to anticipate where their business was heading and how their future needs might be met. They needed to know how the firm was currently being viewed by its clients—not only what they said but what they didn't say, and why they might be turning to its competitors for other products and services. Unfortunately, the self-directed teams never did these things, and consequently they knew only what the customers were telling them about the company's product, not what other products and services they might require for conditions that might be arising in the future, conditions that the customers themselves were only dimly aware of. Thus, the team's perception of what constituted customer satisfaction was critically flawed.

The change effort, therefore, suffered from a number of key problems:

▲ Not everyone involved, especially the leaders, had made the emotional commitment to change. A crucial layer in the change process, one involving the four levers, was completely omitted. As a result, the leaders did not internalize the values of the new culture—that is, they did not adopt a new belief system. (In fact, several of the leaders left partway through the change process.) Nor did they know how to develop a commitment among their subordinates.

▲ The leaders as well as the other employees did not have an opportunity to learn the skills necessary to operate successfully in the new culture.

▲ While empowerment was an important area in which to produce change, it received far too much emphasis, given that there were more important areas, such as customer satisfaction.

▲ There was no alignment of the self-directed teams with the central vision. Instead, the company believed that empowering the parts would

**Figure 9-3. Market penetration of current products.**

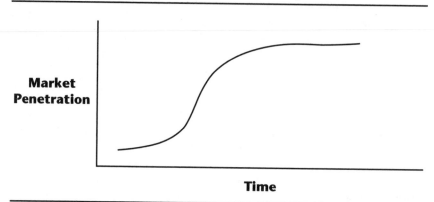

make the whole function effectively. However, without identification with the central vision, the teams lacked a strong set of criteria against which to evaluate what they were doing. There was no integration among the teams, or any glue to hold together the entire change effort. The teams went off in pursuit of their own individual goals. Except for monthly meetings in which the teams discussed their business plans with top management, there was no high-level coordination for the transformation process.

▲ The vision itself was too specific and led to disenchantment among employees when top management was finally forced to step in and reassert control.

▲ The actual process of executing a project (e.g., customer satisfaction) did not begin in the right place, nor did the team members possess the skills needed to carry it out.

## *Making Change Work*

How could this change process have been handled more effectively? First, it had gone companywide and involved all the employees much too early. Instead, the formal and informal leaders should have been won over before the change effort was introduced to the rank and file. To start this process, they might have been presented with the most significant business problem facing the organization. Figure 9-3 shows the position of the company in its current markets.

Over time, its key products had achieved full market penetration and had leveled off. What seemed most critical was to find some new markets for existing products and to develop some new products to introduce into the company's current markets. Once all of the leaders understood the business problem, they could discuss the twelve key areas where change might be necessary, prioritize them, and determine where to begin. For example, customer satisfaction was probably most critical, followed by innovation. These should have received a much higher priority than creating cross-functional teams. The company's vision might also have been much broader and less specific; this could have avoided some of the later disillusionment among employees. Perhaps it would have been enough to say that the company sought to achieve leadership in its field by always making its customers' needs the first priority. This could have been presented in a way that was powerful enough to motivate employees but general enough to avoid problems later on.

This process of setting new priorities might have required a revamping of sales, marketing, and R&D efforts. As a result, a number of leaders would have felt threatened. Despite all the information presented to them about the necessity of change, many might remain firmly committed to the old ways of doing things, and eager to protect their own power and positions. Clearly, the CEO could not fire all of the leaders who might be opposed to the change initiative, although some of the most stubborn resisters might eventually have to go. Instead, he needed to find the proper leverage points and use them to initiate an effective social process to win over the company's leaders.

Remember the new manager of the sales department discussed in Chapters 4 and 6. Although he had a clear vision of what he needed to accomplish, he didn't start there. Data gathering had revealed that his direct reports were already feeling overwhelmed by all the events occurring inside their company, which had just gone through a merger, and were upset because their old boss had just been replaced. The manager faced a dilemma: He could do nothing, in which case the situation inside his department would grow worse, or he could announce his vision and try to initiate change, alienating many of his subordinates and producing more resistance to his change effort. Instead of beginning with his vision, he initiated a social process based upon some key leverage points that involved a clear understanding of human nature. He realized that his subordinates wanted to rebuild their morale and self-esteem. So he started there. As a result, they bonded with him as their leader and became change agents themselves.

A skillful leader knows how to direct the development of a social process that produces the desired change among his or her direct reports. In turn, such leaders must also know how to use the four levers to bring their own subordinates on board. In Chapter 5, for example, we described a social process that enabled a group of consultants in the financial services industry to begin transforming themselves into salespeople. This was a process that involved cracking the employees' old belief system about themselves and their organization and internalizing a new one.

## Using the Four Levers

Every *social process* must begin with a well-defined goal that is clearly communicated by a *persuasive leader.* It should take into account the situation that exists inside the organization and use this situation to provide the energy for change (a crisis, for example, can be an extremely powerful catalyst). As we've already mentioned, the *human needs and feelings* of employees must figure in the design of the social process. A leader must also be aware of the *power dimensions* involving the group members—there may be a cohesive group, for example, or an antinorm group that is resisting change and must be mollified. Finally, a program of activities must be designed and presented in the proper sequence to enable employees to reach the desired goals.

Previously we described the universal solvent, which is a very powerful process that creates momentum and enthusiasm among employees who are embarking on a transformation effort. A social process relies on other components, as well. For example, it may be carefully designed to utilize cognitive dissonance and to create a consensus among its participants, both of which can act as dynamic engines of change. In addition, participants are often asked to make public declarations of support for the leader's vision, which reinforces the feeling of consensus. These are usually highly emotional moments, because a social process, to be effective, must reach employees not only on an intellectual level, but emotionally, too.

This emotional component provides the foundation on which to build employee identification with the change process. Although this is the final element we examined, it is one of the most critical to the entire transformation effort. It helped undermine the change initiative we described in this chapter. Identification involves such things as personal sacrifices by employees, a renunciation of their former behaviors and beliefs, public events and ceremonies to reinforce their commitment to the company's vision, an effective use of symbols to represent new cultural values, and a total dedication to the corporate cause, which employees view as something larger than themselves.

These are the elements that have initiated the great social and political movements of history; they can initiate a great corporate change initiative, as well.

Power is an essential tool in the change effort. A leader uses it to initiate the effort, utilizing an existing crisis or creating one to destabilize the system. Prioritizing the twelve hallmarks, creating a vision and a strategy for implementation, and developing a social process then follow. A leader who understands power can use it to apply pressure on subordinates who stand in the way of change. Powergrams enable a leader to see where the channels of influence lie and how they might be utilized to achieve the leader's goals. If a manager proves resistant to change, a leader might apply pressure from above and below, like the CEO of the toy company who persuaded one of his managers to operate in a team-based culture. As a last resort, a leader might also be forced to fire those managers who will not support the change process and replace them with others who are more amenable to change. What the leader *cannot* do, however, is undertake a change effort if top management is not on board. This is like a general who tries to win a battle while leaving a powerful enemy army in his rear. It simply does not work, and it doomed the change effort we described in this chapter, which went companywide much too early.

This is why the leader must understand the four levers and make them an essential layer of the change process. Not only must the leader utilize the levers with his or her direct reports, they in turn must know how to use these levers with their subordinates to bring them on board in support of the transformation effort. All employees must also identify with the overarching mission of the organization. Finally, employees must be able to master the skills necessary to work in a new environment: team building, greater customer involvement, etc. These are the elements of successful change. It's an extremely complicated process with many different layers. But each is essential if change is to work.

## Follow-Up

Once the change process has been started, it is essential to put procedures in place that can be used to monitor various activities once they are under way. An important element is a mechanism to collect information periodically, certainly no less often than every three months, sampling different levels and different functional areas of the organization, to provide the leader with accurate data. It may not be advisable to trust any internal managers with this undertaking because it is too easy for them to distort the information, and if they do, the data will not provide a true picture of the change effort. Instead, outside consultants might be hired to interview people randomly scattered throughout the firm, collate the results, and report them to the leader. Interview questions should focus on areas such as employee morale, current attitudes toward the change process, buy-in, malfunctions in specific corporate processes, and unexpected events that may have knocked the change effort out of kilter. You wouldn't go on a trip in an unfamiliar country without consulting a map periodically, looking at the road signs along the highway to make sure you're still headed in the right direction, and keeping your eye on the road to avoid any unforeseen obstacles that might suddenly appear along the way. Similar precautions are essential when you set out to transform your organization.

Another key element is to schedule regular meetings with groups of employees at various levels in the organization to reinforce some of the essential parts of the change process. Repetition and reinforcement play a highly instrumental role in retaining momentum and assuring continued commitment from employees. Each meeting might look at some of the following issues: What is the business problem all of us are trying to solve? Which of the twelve key hallmarks are the focus of our efforts? How far along is everyone in improving the situation? What glitches have you, as the leader, become aware of as a result of your information gathering? How are you trying to deal with them? What kind of help do you need from your employees?

No matter how well a change process has been conceptualized, nothing ever runs perfectly. Midcourse corrections will always be necessary, and if these are to work smoothly, you need the support of your employees. That's why the leader must know how to use the four levers skillfully and create identification with the overarching mission of the organization.

The change effort is not a single event that begins and ends in a single year, but a highly complicated process, and it takes a long time for new beliefs and cultural values to be fully inculcated in employees. Remember, change is a struggle for the hearts and minds of human beings—a struggle that never ends.

# Bibliography

**Books**

Argyris, Chris. *Interpersonal Competence and Organizational Effectiveness.* Homewood, Ill.: Irwin, 1962.

———. *Personality and Organization.* New York: Harper, 1957.

Barbash, Fred. *The Founding: A Dramatic Account of the Writing of the Constitution.* New York: Simon & Schuster, 1987.

Bennis, Warren. *On Becoming a Leader.* Reading, Mass.: Addison-Wesley, 1989.

Bloom, Harold, ed. *Modern Critical Interpretations: F. Scott Fitzgerald's "The Great Gatsby."* New York: Chelsea House, 1986.

Bolman, Lee, and Terrence Deal. *Reframing Organizations: Artistry, Choice and Leadership.* San Francisco: Jossey-Bass, 1991.

Bowen, Catherine Drinker. *Miracle at Philadelphia: The Story of the Constitutional Convention, May to September 1787.* Boston: Little Brown, 1966.

Burlingame, Michael. *The Inner World of Abraham Lincoln.* Urbana: University of Illinois, 1994.

Carr, Clay. *Choice, Chance & Organizational Change: Practical Thoughts From Evolution for Business Leaders & Thinkers.* New York: AMACOM, 1996.

Conger, Jay. *Learning to Lead: The Art of Transforming Managers Into Leaders.* San Francisco: Jossey-Bass, 1992.

Deal, Terrence, and Allen Kennedy. *Corporate Cultures.* Reading, Mass.: Addison-Wesley, 1982.

Dos Passos, John. *Mr. Wilson's War.* Garden City, N.Y.: Doubleday, 1962.

Eccles, Robert, and Nitin Nohria. *Beyond the Hype: Rediscovering the Essence of Management.* Boston: Harvard Business School Press, 1992.

Erickson, Carolly. *Our Tempestuous Day: A History of Regency England.* New York: Morrow, 1986.

Felsham, Neil. *Gorbachev, Yeltsin and the Last Days of the Soviet Empire.* New York: St. Martin's, 1992.

165

Festinger, Leon, Henry W. Riecken, and Stanley Schacter. *When Prophecy Fails*. New York: Harper, 1964.

Hackman, Richard, ed. *Groups That Work (and Those That Don't): Creating Conditions for Effective Teamwork*. San Francisco: Jossey-Bass, 1990.

Hammer, Michael, and James Champy. *Reengineering the Corporation*. New York: HarperCollins, 1993.

Harrison, John. *Quest for the New Moral World: Robert Owen and the Owenites in Britain and America*. New York: Scribner's, 1969.

Heller, Robert. *The Super Chiefs*. New York: Dutton, 1992.

Hill, Linda A. *Becoming a Manager: Mastery of a New Identity*. Boston: Harvard Business School Press, 1992.

Horton, Thomas. *The CEO Paradox: The Privilege and Accountability of Leadership*. New York: AMACOM, 1992.

Ingrassia, Paul, and Joseph B. White. *Comeback: The Fall and Rise of the American Automobile Industry*. New York: Simon & Schuster, 1994.

Ketchum, Ralph. *James Madison: A Biography*. New York: Macmillan, 1971.

Kets de Vries, Manfred. *Prisoners of Leadership*. New York: Wiley, 1989.

Kotter, John. *The General Managers*. New York: Free Press, 1982.

―――. *Power and Influence*. New York: Free Press, 1985.

―――. *The Leadership Factor*. New York: Free Press, 1988.

―――. *Corporate Culture and Performance*. New York: Free Press, 1992.

Marshall, Edward. *Transforming the Way We Work: The Power of the Collaborative Workplace*. New York: AMACOM, 1995.

Mills, D. Quinn. *Rebirth of the Corporation*. New York: Wiley, 1991.

Mohrman, Allan, et al. *Large-Scale Organizational Change*. San Francisco: Jossey-Bass, 1990.

Mosley, Leonard. *Marshall: Hero for Our Times*. New York: Hearst, 1982.

Neustadt, Richard, and Ernest May. *Thinking in Time*. New York: Free Press, 1986.

Petersen, Donald, and John Hillkirk. *A Better Idea: Redefining the Ways Americans Work*. Boston: Houghton Mifflin, 1991.

Pinchot, Gifford, and Elizabeth Pinchot. *The End of Bureaucracy and the Rise of the Intelligent Organization*. San Francisco: Berrett-Koehler, 1993.

Potts, Mark, and Peter Behr. *The Leading Edge: CEOs Who Turned Their Companies Around*. New York: McGraw-Hill, 1987.

Quick, James C., Debra Nelson, and Jonathan Quick. *Stress and Challenge at the Top: The Paradox of the Successful Executive*. New York: Wiley, 1990.

Rosen, Robert. *The Healthy Company: Eight Strategies to Develop People, Productivity, and Profits*. Los Angeles: J. P. Tarcher, 1991.

Sears, Stephen W. *To the Gates of Richmond: The Peninsula Campaign*. New York: Ticknor & Fields, 1992.

Senge, Peter. *The Fifth Discipline*. New York: Doubleday, 1990.

Sheehy, Gail. *The Man Who Changed the World*. New York: HarperCollins, 1990.

Smith, Gene. *When the Cheering Stopped: The Last Years of Woodrow Wilson*. New York: Morrow, 1964.

Smith, Kerwyn K. *Groups in Conflict*. Dubuque, Iowa: Kendall/Hunt, 1982.

Syrett, Michael, and Clare Hogg, eds. *Frontiers of Leadership*. Cambridge, Mass.: Blackwell, 1992.

Tichy, Noel, and Stratford Sherman. *Control Your Destiny or Someone Else Will*. New York: HarperCollins, 1993.

Tomasko, Robert. *Rethinking the Corporation: The Architecture of Change*. New York: AMACOM, 1995.

Tuchman, Barbara. *The March of Folly: From Troy to Vietnam*. New York: Knopf, 1984.

Waterman, Robert H., Jr. *What America Does Right: Learning From Companies That Put People First*. New York: Norton, 1994.

Watson, James. *As I Knew Them: Memoirs of James E. Watson*. Indianapolis: Bobbs-Merrill, 1936.

Webber, Everett. *Escape to Utopia: The Communal Movement in America*. New York: Hastings House, 1959.

Zimmerman, Frederick. *The Turnaround Experience: Real World Lessons in Revitalizing Corporations*. New York: McGraw-Hill, 1991.

### Articles

Beer, Michael, Russell Eisenstat, and Bert Spector. "Why Change Programs Don't Produce Change." *Harvard Business Review,* Nov.–Dec. 1990, 158–66.

Bryant, Adam. "One Big Happy Family No More." *New York Times*, March 22, 1995, D1.

Byrne, John, Kathleen Kerwin, Amy Cortese, and Paula Dwyer. "Borderless Management." *Business Week*, May 23, 1994, 24–26.

Duck, Jeanie. "Managing Change: The Art of Balancing." *Harvard Business Review,* Nov.–Dec. 1993, 109–18.

Dumaine, Brian. "The Trouble With Teams." *Fortune*, Sept. 5, 1994, 86–92.

Filipczak, Bob. "You're on Your Own: Training, Employability, and the New Employee Contract." *Training*, January 1995, 29–36.

Fisher, Anne. "Making Change Stick." *Fortune*, April 17, 1995, 121–28.

Gordon, Jack. "The Team Troubles That Won't Go Away." *Training*, August 1994, 25–34.

Greising, David. "Quality: Making It Pay." *Business Week*, Aug. 8, 1994, 54–59.

Hahn, Robert. "How Tough Is It to Be a College President?" *The Chronicle of Higher Education*, Jan. 6, 1995, A64.

Hamilton, Martha. "An Elephant Slims Down to Battle the Gazelles: DuPont's Fitness Program Is Paying Off." *Washington Post National Weekly*, Aug. 29–Sept. 4, 1994, 22.

Hammer, Michael. "Reengineering Work: Don't Automate, Obliterate." *Harvard Business Review*, July–August 1990, 104–11.

Hogan, Robert, Gordon Curphy, and Joyce Hogan. "What We Know About Leadership." *American Psychologist*, June 1994, 493–504.

Huey, John. "Managing in the Midst of Chaos." *Fortune*, April 5, 1993, 40–48.

Kelly, Kevin, and Peter Burrows. "Motorola: Training for the Millenium." *Business Week*, March 28, 1994, 158–63.

Labich, Kenneth. "Why Companies Fail." *Fortune*, Nov. 14, 1994, 52–68.

Levin, Doron. "Joe Montana, A Study in Good Management." *New York Times*, Jan. 23, 1994, F11.

Mitchell, Russell, and Michael O'neal. "Managing by Values: Is Levi Strauss' Approach Visionary—or Flaky?" *Business Week*, Aug. 1, 1994, 46–51.

Shapiro, Benson, Adrian Slywotzky, and Richard Tedlow. "Why Great Companies Go Wrong." *New York Times*, Nov. 6, 1994, F11.

———. "Managing in a Wired Company." *Fortune*, July 11, 1991, 45–50.

Smith, Lee. "Burned-Out Bosses." *Fortune*, July 25, 1994, 42–52.

Stewart, Thomas. "Rate Your Readiness to Change." *Fortune*, Feb. 7, 1994, 106–12.

Taylor, Alex. "Iacocca's Minivan." *Fortune*, May 30, 1994, 56–66.

# Index